Treating Victims of Mass Disaster and Terrorism

About the Authors

Jennifer Housley, MS, is active in local, national, and international organizations addressing the psychological consequences of trauma. Currently at the Pacific Graduate School of Psychology and National Center on the Psychology of Terrorism in Palo Alto, California, she has served as Program Director for the Palo Alto Medical Reserve Corps and published on topics related to mass disaster, trauma, and health psychology. She is a widely respected advisor, program developer, and instructor on interventions, coping, and first aid following trauma and disaster, both for licensed mental health professionals and for first responders and disaster volunteers.

Larry E. Beutler, PhD is Distinguished Professor, Chair, and former Director of Training at the Pacific Graduate School of Psychology in Palo Alto, California and is a Consulting Professor of Psychiatry at Stanford University School of Medicine. Dr. Beutler is the former Editor of the *Journal of Clinical Psychology* and of the *Journal of Consulting and Clinical Psychology*. He is a fellow of the American Psychological Association and the American Psychological Society. He is the Past-President of the Society for Clinical Psychology (Division 12 of APA), a Past President of the Division of Psychotherapy (APA), and a two-term Past-President of the (International) Society for Psychotherapy Research. He is the author of approximately 300 scientific papers and chapters, and is the author, editor or coauthor of fourteen books on psychotherapy and psychopathology.

Advances in Psychotherapy – Evidence-Based Practice

Danny Wedding; PhD, MPH, Prof., St. Louis, MO
(Series Editor)
Larry Beutler; PhD, Prof., Palo Alto, CA
Kenneth E. Freedland; PhD, Prof., St. Louis, MO
Linda C. Sobell; PhD, ABPP, Prof., Ft. Lauderdale, FL
David A. Wolfe; PhD, Prof., Toronto
(Associate Editors)

The basic objective of this new series is to provide therapists with practical, evidence-based treatment guidance for the most common disorders seen in clinical practice – and to do so in a "reader-friendly" manner. Each book in the series is both a compact "how-to-do" reference on a particular disorder for use by professional clinicians in their daily work, as well as an ideal educational resource for students and for practice-oriented continuing education.

The most important feature of the books is that they are practical and "reader-friendly": All are structured similarly and all provide a compact and easy-to-follow guide to all aspects that are relevant in real-life practice. Tables, boxed clinical "pearls", marginal notes, and summary boxes assist orientation, while checklists provide tools for use in daily practice.

Treating Victims of Mass Disaster and Terrorism

WITHDRAWN

Jennifer Housley
Pacific Graduate School of Psychology, Palo Alto, CA

Larry E. Beutler
Pacific Graduate School of Psychology, Palo Alto, CA

HOGREFE

Library of Congress Cataloging in Publication

is available via the Library of Congress Marc Database under the
LC Control Number 2006930641

Library and Archives Canada Cataloguing in Publication

Housley, Jennifer
   Treating victims of mass disaster and terrorism / Jennifer Housley and Larry E. Beutler.

(Advances in psychotherapy--evidence-based practice)
Includes bibliographical references.
ISBN 0-88937-321-3

   1. Disaster victims--Mental health. 2. Victims of terrorism--Mental health.
3. Disaster victims--Rehabilitation. 4. Victims of terrorism--Rehabilitation.
5. Psychic trauma--Treatment. I. Beutler, Larry E. II. Title. III. Series.

RC552.P67H68 2006   616.85'21   C2006-903902-X

PUBLISHING OFFICES
USA: Hogrefe & Huber Publishers, 875 Massachusetts Avenue, 7th Floor,
               Cambridge, MA 02139
               Phone (866) 823-4726, Fax (617) 354-6875; E-mail info@hhpub.com
EUROPE: Hogrefe & Huber Publishers, Rohnsweg 25, 37085 Göttingen, Germany
               Phone +49 551 49609-0, Fax +49 551 49609-88, E-mail hh@hhpub.com

SALES & DISTRIBUTION
USA: Hogrefe & Huber Publishers, Customer Services Department,
               30 Amberwood Parkway, Ashland, OH 44805
               Phone (800) 228-3749, Fax (419) 281-6883, E-mail custserv@hhpub.com
EUROPE: Hogrefe & Huber Publishers, Rohnsweg 25, 37085 Göttingen, Germany
               Phone +49 551 49609-0, Fax +49 551 49609-88, E-mail hh@hhpub.com

OTHER OFFICES
CANADA: Hogrefe & Huber Publishers, 1543 Bayview Avenue, Toronto, Ontario M4G 3B5
SWITZERLAND: Hogrefe & Huber Publishers, Länggass-Strasse 76, CH-3000 Bern 9

Hogrefe & Huber Publishers
Incorporated and registered in the State of Washington, USA, and in Göttingen, Lower Saxony,
Germany

Printed and bound in the USA
ISBN 10: 0-88937-321-3
ISBN 13: 978-0-88937-321-1

Preface

This book represents the integration of work conducted by a task force jointly sponsored by the Society of Clinical Psychology (Division 12 of the American Psychological Association, APA) and the North American Society for Psychotherapy Research (NASPR) with treatment tools for survivors of mass trauma events. Specifically, this book introduces the concept of using the principles of therapeutic changes identified by this Task Force as a framework for staged treatment for mass-trauma survivors. This approach is offered to the reader as one of many potential alternatives that are available for use in their efforts to address the needs of mass trauma survivors.

Given the preponderance of recent disasters, we find ourselves in a time when many mental health care professionals throughout the world are working to determine what approaches may be the most efficient and effective in assisting survivors. We acknowledge that there are many varied approaches available at this time and anticipate even more being available in the future. Our hope is that this program will serve as a contribution to these efforts, inspire additional ideas, and will be a foundation from which additional work can grow. We do not profess to have all the answers, but the following text offers to you some of our thoughts, intended to be of use to you in your disaster response efforts.

Acknowledgments

Work on this volume was supported in part by a Medical Reserve Corps (MRC) grant to James Breckenridge, PhD, in Palo Alto, CA. Larry E. Beutler, PhD, served as Director and Coinvestigator of the Palo Alto MRC Project and Jennifer Housley, MS, served as the Program Director. Our thanks are extended to Dr. Breckenridge for his ongoing support. The authors also wish to acknowledge and thank Josef Ruzek, PhD,. for his valuable contributions to this book. We would also like to acknowledge those professionals, both researchers and providers, who have dedicated so much of their resources and energy in growing the knowledge base of disaster response and trauma intervention. We are grateful to our peers at the Pacific Graduate School of Psychology who have provided us ongoing encouragement and support.

Consistent with our recommendations to thank those who have made our efforts possible (see Self-Care and Coping section), we would also like to extend our gratitude to our family and friends (specifically to Mr. Patrick Patterson, Ms. Mary Housley, and Ms. Jamie Beutler) for their encouragement, support, and tolerance of our work not only on this volume but also of our involvement in disaster response.

This effort is dedicated to the late Mr. Richard Housley for his everlasting love, knowledge, and wisdom that continue to bring light, comfort, and integrity to so many journeys. Mr. Housley recommended always doing "the best you can with what you've got at the time." There may be few ways to better summarize our ongoing efforts in the disaster response field.

Table of Contents

1

Description

1.1 Terminology

Unlike many treatments that are described both in this series and under the heading of "empirically supported" or "research-based" treatments, the intervention described in this volume does not focus on individuals by diagnostic classification. The treatment of survivors and first responders who have been exposed to mass trauma, and particularly to terrorism is defined by the event, not by a specific form of psychopathological response. While most people who are exposed to mass trauma, including terrorist trauma, will experience acute stress disorder (ASD) during the immediate postevent process, as time goes on, a wide variety of responses occur, including a return to normal functioning.

Treatment is defined by the event not by a specific form of psychopathological response

People are surprisingly resilient, and a substantial majority of those exposed will not warrant a mental health diagnosis at all, beyond the immediate postevent period. Thus, to focus on a specific syndrome, like posttraumatic stress disorder (PTSD), is both to assume a degree of homogeneity of response that is not present following mass trauma and to miss the variety of problems presented. Moreover, basing a treatment on exclusionary consideration of a single diagnostic condition will fail adequately to address the needs of many, if not most, of those who are needy of services and whose postadjustment is characterized by such syndromes as major depression and chemical abuse/ dependence, family disruption, and generalized anxiety. Thus, the treatment of survivors of terrorism and disasters must be broadly conceived and easily adaptable to a variety of patient conditions over a substantial period of time.

Treatment must be broadly conceived and easily adaptable

1.2 Definition

Because this book does not focus on a specific disorder, but rather on the broad range of psychological consequences that follow a terrorist-initiated event (or other mass casualty events), there is not a singular definition that can be provided of the disorder and problem to be treated. It is most efficient to characterize reactions to traumatic events through differing stress reactions (i.e., consequences). These consequences include those reactions normally associated with ASD and PTSD but also include other reactions. These other effects include any temporary or long-term, adverse psychological reactions that are stimulated by the trauma (e.g., use of negative coping in an effort to avoid memories or emotions through increased substance use, major depression, chemical dependence, etc.).

ASD, PTSD, depression and substance abuse are some of the psychological reactions to disaster

One of the most pervasive and consistent reactions to mass trauma is that of ASD, which is prevalent during the early, postevent period. But, for most people, this syndrome dissipates with time, even without specific treatment. ASD is but the nucleus of symptoms from which a variety of posttrauma reactions may evolve.

PTSD, depression, and chemical abuse are the diagnoses most often seen among postterror and posttrauma survivors, and generally are considered to be stress-induced (e.g., Galea, Ahern, Resnick et al., 2002; Galea, Vlahov, Resnick et al., 2003). A host of other, nonsyndromal, stress-related problems are likely to also manifest themselves in response to terrorist events, however, and many of these require or are likely to be responsive to treatment. These problems may range from specific symptoms of depression and chemical abuse to vague symptoms of anxiety and family disruption.

1.3   Epidemiology

Unfortunately, it is difficult to obtain accurate and reliable base rate data on minor and subclinical, stress-related conditions. The most accurate epidemiological picture of response to the specific case of a terrorist attack comes from mapping the incidence and prevalence rates observed among those who have been exposed to terrorism or other mass trauma onto the base-rates of stress-induced conditions of ASD, PTSD, major depression, and chemical abuse that existed previously in the observed population. The mental health impact of terrorist/mass trauma events can be estimated as the degree to which stress-induced conditions are increased above normative expectations, following a terrorist event. The best estimates of normative expectations for these comparisons are derived from three sources.

The Epidemiologic Catchment Area Study (Narrow et al., 2002; Regier et al., 1998; Robins, Locke, & Regier, 1991), conducted by the National Institute of Mental Health, extracted census-based samples at five sites between 1980 and 1985. Over 20,000 individuals over the age of 18 were surveyed. The National Comorbidity Study (NCS; Kessler et al., 1997) was initiated a few years later in response to a congressional mandate to identify the prevalence of mental health and substance abuse disorders which could then serve as the basis for establishing a national policy for the treatment of mental health and drug abuse disorders. A partial replication of this latter survey (NCS-R; Kessler, Chiu et al., 2005; Kessler, Demler et al., 2005) was conducted about 10 years later, between 2000 and 2003, to replicate the NCS study and to determine changes in incidence and prevalence rates of various disorders.

There are several important methodological differences in how these surveys were conducted. These differences, compounded with changes in the diagnostic system and the introduction of ASD in 1994, with the advent of DSM-IV, resulted in some significant disparities among the ECS and NCS surveys, particularly in estimates of lifetime rates of various disorders. Nonetheless, there is reasonable consistency among the reports on the 12-month incidence rates of trauma-induced disorders (ASD, PTSD, depression, chemical abuse). Supplemented by some specialized and continuing surveys of specific problems (e.g., the Household Survey on Drug Abuse by SAMHSA, 2002; surveys following the events of September 11, 2001), a reasonable estimate is possible of the impact of mass terrorism.

Combining the results of the initial ECA report (Regier et al., 1998 and the two NCS reports (Kessler et al., 1994; Kessler et al., 2005), the probable, 12-month prevalence rate of PTSD/ASD in the general population is about 8%. The risk rate for women is about twice that of men (10% versus 5%); among men, African-American males are at greatest risk. However, in all likelihood, the observed sex and ethnic differences are reflections of varying social roles, intensity of prior exposure to violence, and contexts rather than being reflections of inherent biological vulnerabilities (Galea, Vlahav, & Resnick, 2003).

Women are twice as much at risk of PTSD than men

Prevalence rates of depression are somewhat more variable in the demographic, normative surveys than are rates of PTSD/ASD in the normative samples. Lifetime prevalence rates of depression vary from 8% in the ECA survey to 19% in the NCS survey, with 12-month rates being somewhat more consistent and hovering near 10% (Beutler, Clarkin, & Bongar, 2000). Adding the prevalence rates of comorbid and non-comorbid chemical abuse, which hover around 10%, results in a general population baseline, 12-month risk of between 22% and 24%. This is the expected rate, within a nonterrorism-exposed population, of having the symptoms that are the most likely to be affected and exacerbated by a mass terror-initiated event.

Against this base rate, one can compare the prevalence rates of these same stress-induced disorders in the New York City area, following the terrorism-initiated events of 9/11/01. It is uncertain how generalizable the resulting estimates of terrorist impact are, however. It is likely that they are culture and region/country specific because of wide variations in the frequency of exposure and cultural beliefs about terrorism that characterizes the responses of survivors from different areas and cultures. For our purposes, we will compare the baseline rates observed in the three U.S. surveys to the rates of problems present among those people who were most directly exposed to mass terrorism on September 11, 2001.

Random surveys of residents of the New York City area following 9/11 have typically concluded that there has been an increase in mental health problems generally, in this region, especially among those most directly exposed to terrorism. However, actual demonstration that the post 9/11 prevalence is higher than the normative base rate expectations has been hard to come by, and estimates of actual incidence rates have varied widely among surveys. Population-based surveys have suggested slightly higher rates of PTSD-like symptoms than those surveys that have relied on less direct assessment methods (Galea, Ahern, Resnick et al., 2002). Nonetheless, it seems quite clear that symptoms of ASD during the first month following a mass trauma event affect most of the exposed population, and it is also clear that there is a high rate of general recovery even in untreated populations, over the following 6 months. Thus, somewhat surprisingly, diagnosable PTSD (which, by definition, can only be present after a month or more following the incident event) was not demonstrably different than the expected normative rates in the New York City area, within about six months of 9/11/2001. The data suggest that the greatest increases of stress-induced problems were in the areas of depression and chemical abuse, rather than in PTSD. Even here, however, it is uncertain how large the increased risk actually might be. The most careful estimates suggest that over a six-month period, the overall risk of behavioral and emotional disorders was increased by about 10% (e.g., Galea, Vlahov, Resnick et al., 2003; Schuster, Stein et al., 2001; Vlahav, Galea, Resnick et al., 2002; Fairbrother, Stuber, Galea et al., 2003).

1.4   Course and Prognosis

Stress reactions are to be expected following a mass trauma event such as a terrorist attack. In fact, Friedman, Hamblen, Foa, and Charney (2004) report that one third of survivors of high impact disasters experience clinically significant distress, that those who express such symptoms in the early postdisaster time frame are at greatest risk for long-term impairment, and that delayed onset is rare. Nonetheless, there is a rapid recovery and relief of most of the early symptoms of distress. Thus, prognosis for recovery is good to excellent, even among untreated survivors. A substantial portion of victims do, however, have continuing and long-term problems. Predicting who will experience these is a continuing problem. There are a variety of predictors that have been investigated.

Most people recover from early symptoms of distress without assistance

Proximity of exposure has been consistently related to the severity or subsequent symptoms. Proximity is defined as either by direct physical exposure or by being indirectly exposed through one's relationships with survivors. However, even the influence of proximal exposure is moderated by the reported levels of previous exposure to trauma, one's prior psychiatric status, and by availability of social support networks (Galea, Resnick, Ahern et al., 2002; Galea, Vlahov, Resnick et al., 2003). The role of multiple exposure to trauma is especially important, and among those who are repeatedly exposed, such as combat veterans, the prevalence rates of stress reactions are about double (+30%) that of those exposed to a single, major stressor (Kulka, Schlenger, & Fairbank, 1990).

The presence of ASD symptoms is not a reliable predictor of long-term problems

High levels of acute stress reactions may also predict development of PTSD. Bryant (2003), in his review of studies testing the predictive power of an ASD diagnosis, reports that a portion of people who exhibit ASD within one month posttrauma develop PTSD. However, the majority of those who have ASD symptoms improve over the course of the intervening month and many who develop PTSD have not experienced a full complement of ASD symptoms. Thus, the presence of ASD symptoms immediately following the incident event may not be a reliable predictor of long-term problems (e.g., Friedman et al., 2004).

The presence of negative versus positive cognitions following traumatic events may also assist providers in determining who may be at risk of developing PTSD as positive cognitions may be associated with resilience (Friedman et al., 2004). Additional means by which to distinguish potentially resilient survivors may include the presence of accurate encoding, processing, and trauma memory retrieval early in the posttrauma period (Harvey, Bryant, & Dung, 1998; Moulds & Bryant 2002; Friedman et al., 2004). It is also important to note that avoidance, though one of the many symptoms associated with ASD and PTSD, may actually serve an adaptive role in the early stages posttrauma (Ehlers & Steil, 1995; Friedman et al., 2004). Other factors likely to contribute to resiliency are high versus low cognitive ability and high versus low levels of social support (McNally, Bryant, & Ehlers, 2004).

Dissociative symptoms have also been investigated as predictors of PTSD. The results of these studies, however, are not entirely clear. For example, some researchers have found dissociation to have no additional predictive power beyond symptoms of reexperiencing, avoidance, and hyperarousal (Brewin, Andrews, Rose, & Kirk, 1999; Marshall & Schell, 2002; McNally et al., 2004) while others have found evidence that dissociation does carry predictive power (e.g., Murray et al., 2002; McNally et al., 2004).

Table 1 summarizes some of the current literature on predictors of long-term difficulties following an incident event. It is important to note that not all risk factors are consistent across studies and that the measures used, type of trauma experienced by participants, and populations sampled differ as well. This table illustrates the wide variety of risk factors associated with the development of PTSD and gives the provider a conceptual understanding of *red flags* that may alert them to whether referrals may be warranted. It is obviously premature to proclaim that at-risk individuals can be identified with great accuracy, but using this type of information as a general guide, the provider may be able to make better educated decisions regarding referral and treatment for individuals following a mass trauma event when using this proposed 3-stage program.

There are some potential predictors for long-term difficulties that are also red-flags for the next stage of treatment

Collectively, one can conclude that with or without treatment, a large percentage of survivors do not qualify for an Axis I psychiatric diagnosis by the end of six-months following a traumatic incident (e.g., Galea, Resnick, Ahern et al., 2002; Galea, Vlahov, Resnick et al., 2003). Some, however, will continue to experience anxiety symptoms. There is also the possibility that some will have delayed reactions, even though these concerns have not been demonstrated to be warranted in extant research. While constant exploration of these possibilities is necessary, the pressing focus of any intervention must be to identify those who are at long-term risk as soon as possible, and to intervene with these individuals in the hope that by doing so we may reduce the rates of long-term effects among vulnerable groups.

The first problem facing those who seek to develop an effective treatment is identifying those who should be treated. Unfortunately, the relationship of prognostic predictors to treatment effectiveness is unclear, and the relationships between prognostic predictors and actual risk are weak. Without clearly being able to identify those who present a long-term risk, it may not be cost-effective to institute broad-ranging and inclusive treatment programs, especially early in the postevent period. Such programs result in treating many people who will recover without specific intervention. Additionally, such programs applied to everyone may come at the cost of actually slowing the natural course of recovery. For example, the most frequently used treatment during the initial period, immediately following a mass traumatic event, Critical Incident Stress Debriefing (CISD; Beutler et al., 2006; Gist & Lubin, 1999; Litz & Gray, 2004), has been shown to slow down the natural course of recovery among a substantial proportion (perhaps as many as 20%) of survivors (e.g., Litz et al., 2002; McNally et al., 2003; Rose et al., 1998; Rose et al., 1999).

Research suggests that use of the CISD may actually slow the natural recovery process

Table 1
Predictors of Risk

Identified predictor or risk factor	Reference
Resource loss and depression act as superior predictors of psychological distress than a sense of coherence and anxiety	Kaiser, Sattler, & Bellack (1996)
In their review of 160 studies involving disaster victims, Friedman et al. determined that individual level risk factors for poor mental health outcome following disaster include: severity of exposure, personal characteristics (such as female gender, low socioeconomic status, previous psychiatric history, little previous disaster exposure), family context (including child caring responsibilities for females, parental distress for children, significant distress by any family member), and resource loss.	Friedman, Hamblen, Foa, & Charney (2004) (review article)
Predictors of PTSD are reported as Hispanic ethnicity, 2 or more prior stressors, occurrence of panic attack during or immediately postterrorist attack, proximity to disaster location, and event-caused loss of possessions.	Galea, Ahern, Resnick, Kilpatrick, Bucuvalas, Gold, & Vlahov (2002)
Predictors of depression are reported as Hispanic ethnicity, 2 or more stressors, a panic attack, low level of social support, death of friend or relative, or loss of job resulting from terrorist attacks.	Galea et al. (2002)
Dysfunctional cognitions (e.g., world as completely dangerous place and viewing self as incompetent) proposed to mediate development and maintenance of PTSD	Foa & Cahill (2001); Friedman et al. (2004)
Negative cognitions about self and the world and self-blame correlated with measures of PTSD severity, depression, and general anxiety	Foa, Ehlers, Clark, Tolin, & Orsillo (1999)
Cognitive processing style (mental defeat, mental confusion, detachment), appraisal of assault sequelae (appraisal of symptoms, perceived negative responses of others, permanent change), negative beliefs about self and world, and maladaptive control strategies (avoidance/safety seeking) as variables predicting PTSD at both 6 and 9 month follow-ups postphysical or sexual assault	Dumore, Clark, & Ehlers (2001); McNally et al. (2003)
Perceived threat as predictor of PTSD	Kilpatrick, Veronen, & Resick (1982); Friedman et al. (2004)
Negative expectations about the impact (both immediate and long-term) of the traumatic event as predictor of PTSD	Bryant (2003); McNally et al. (2003); Friedman et al. (2004)

Table 1 (continued)

Identified predictor or risk factor	Reference
Sense of personal incompetence and loss of sanity as predictors of PTSD	Ehlers & Clark (2000); McNally et al. (2003); Friedman et al., (2004)
Prior exposure to trauma	King, King, Foy, Keane, & Fairbank (1999); Litz et al. (2002)
Indicates that risk of PTSD may be increased by effects of female gender, greater social, educational, and intellectual disadvantages, individual and family psychiatric history, previous adversity, and childhood abuse	Brewin, Andrews, & Valentine (2000)
Posttrauma shame, guilt, and self-blame following the trauma as predictors of PTSD	Andrews, Brewin, Rose, & Kirk (2000); McNally et al. (2003); Friedman et al. (2004)
Posttrauma (1 to 2 weeeks and onward) symptom severity; depersonalization, emotional numbing, motor restlessness and a sense of reliving the trauma as measured within 1 month posttrauma as predictor of PTSD	Harvey & Bryant (1998); McNally et al. (2003)
Peri-traumatic dissociation as predictor of PTSD	Ozer, Best, Lipsey, & Weiss (2003); McNally et al. (2003)
Cognitive ability as predictor of PTSD	Vasterling, Brailey, & Constans, (1997); McNally et al. (2003)
Peri-traumatic dissociation measured at 4 weeks posttrauma was a better predictor than persistent dissociation measured at 1-week posttrauma of PTSD at 6 months posttrauma	Murray, Ehlers, & Mayou (2002); McNally et al. (2003)
Derealization and sense of time distortion at 1-week posttrauma as predictors of PTSD 6-months posttrauma	Shalev, Peri Canetti, & Schrieber, (1996); McNally et al. (2003)
Potential for acute psychophysiological arousal as mediator of PTSD (long-term)	Bryant, Harvey, Guthrie, & Moulds (2003)

The National Institute for Clinical Excellence (2005) recommends that "for individuals who have experienced a traumatic event, the systematic provision to that individual alone of brief, single-session interventions (often referred to as debriefing) that focus on the traumatic incident, should not be routine practice when delivering services" (p. 4).

1.5   Differential Diagnosis

For the purposes of this book, differential diagnosis is defined as the processes by which one can differentiate among those conditions that are initiated by a mass traumatic event and those that are preexistent or that are initiated by some other event.

The major conditions that are initiated by a mass traumatic event include ASD, PTSD, major depression, and chemical abuse or dependence. Additional, more transitory symptoms (e.g., sleep disorder, general anxiety, adjustment disorder, etc.) may also occur following trauma. These conditions may also occur from events other than a mass trauma, and in some cases may be observed in the absence of any identifiable traumatic event (e.g., major depression, chemical abuse). However, for the purposes of this treatment program, all symptoms and conditions within these spectra are considered to be available for treatment using this protocol, if they arise subsequent to a mass trauma, especially one that is initiated by a terrorist event. Symptoms and disorders that arise following a terrorist-initiated event but that did not exist prior to the event in the same form are defined by the nature of the event and the individual's reaction to the event.

It is helpful to review disorders that share symptoms similar to those seen following mass casualty events

Though the approach taken by this volume does not seek to address specific disorders, it is helpful to review disorders that share symptoms similar to those seen following mass casualty events. The following descriptions are derived from the *DSM-IV-TR* (American Psychiatric Association, 2001). The descriptions provided are intended for informational purposes only and the reader is encouraged to consult the *DSM-IV-TR* for more detailed information regarding symptoms and diagnostic criteria.

1.5.1   Posttraumatic Stress Disorder (PTSD)

To diagnose someone with PTSD, the individual must have had exposure to a traumatic event that involved real or perceived threat to self or others. The individual must also experience one or more symptoms of reexperiencing, three or more symptoms of avoidance/numbing, and two or more symptoms of increased arousal. These symptoms, in addition to significant distress in life functioning, must be present for more than one month.

1.5.2   Acute Stress Disorder (ASD)

ASD shares a variety of symptoms with PTSD. The difference between ASD and PTSD is primarily a temporal one. For ASD, symptoms must be present for a minimum of 2 days and a maximum of 4 weeks and must occur within 1 month of the traumatic event. There are also less strict criteria as to the number of symptoms experienced within each category. The person must have experienced at least three symptoms of dissociation, one or more persistent reexperiencing symptoms, exhibit marked avoidance and increased arousal, and experience significant distress in life functioning. In addition, the client's symptoms must not be due to substance use or a general medical condition.

1.5.3 Other Anxiety Disorders

As previously mentioned, a variety of anxiety-related symptoms are common following a significant traumatic event. To diagnose specific anxiety disorders additional criteria must be met. Anxiety disorders such as panic disorder with or without agoraphobia and generalized anxiety disorder share symptoms with those commonly seen after trauma exposure. For panic disorder with agoraphobia, the individual must experience recurrent unexpected panic attacks. These attacks must be followed by one month of one or more of either persistent concern about having more attacks, concern about the implication of an attack, and/or a significant behavioral change related to such attacks. In both cases, whether agoraphobia is present or not, the panic attacks must not be due to substance use or a general medical condition. For GAD, the individual must express excessive anxiety and worry for more days than not for at least six months. The worry must be difficult to control, and be associated with a range of other symptoms such as fatigue, irritability, difficulty concentration, tension, and sleep disturbance.

1.5.4 Major Depressive Disorder

A major depressive episode is characterized by the presence of five or more symptoms being present within a 2 week period where at least one of the symptoms is depressed mood or loss of interest or pleasure. These symptoms include depressed mood for the majority of the day, diminished pleasure in activities nearly everyday, significant weight change, sleep disturbances, psychomotor agitation or retardation, fatigue, feelings of worthlessness or guilt, and decreased ability to concentrate. These symptoms must not be due to substance use or a general medical condition. Major depressive disorder can be diagnosed as single episode or recurrent. To be considered as recurrent, there must be two or more depressive episodes that must be spaced out by at least 2 consecutive months.

1.5.5 Sleep Disorders

A variety of symptoms associated with sleep disorders are common among the reactions seen following traumatic events. These include dyssomnia's such as primary insomnia. Primary hypersomnia, dyssomnia not otherwise specified, and parasomnia's such as nightmare disorder, sleep terror disorder, and substance-induced sleep disorder. For dyssomnia's, symptoms must be present for one month (or less if recurrent). To diagnose nightmare disorder, the nightmares must not be attributable to PTSD, substance or general medical condition. For sleep terror disorder, the individual must not be able to recall the dream in detail or respond to others' efforts to comfort them during the terror, nor can the symptoms be due to substance use or a general medical condition.

1.5.6   Adjustment Disorders

Diagnoses of adjustment disorder requires a change in behavior or emotion that occurs within three months of the onset of an identifiable stressor. It is important to note that once the stressor is over, the symptoms must not continue for more than six months. A diagnosis of chronic adjustment disorder can be made if the symptoms last more than six months and are in response to a chronic stressor or one that has ongoing consequences.

1.5.7   Substance Related Disorders

Substance disorders include both substance dependence and substance abuse. Substance dependence requires that the individual exhibit a maladaptive pattern of abuse that leads to impairment. Within 12 months, three or more symptoms must be present. These symptoms include tolerance, withdrawal, taken in larger amounts or over longer time periods than intended, desire or failed efforts to reduce intake, spending a large portion of time attaining substance, decreased participation in social, job-related, or recreational activities, and continued use despite continued risk for physical or psychological harm to ensue. Substance abuse is characterized by recurrent and maladaptive substance use patterns that impair the individuals ability to meet expectations associated with work, school, or home activities, use that puts the individual or others at risk for harm (including legal problems), and continued use despite potential or actual problems.

1.6   Comorbidities

Aside from distinguishing among the foregoing disorders and conditions, the reaction to extreme trauma is complicated by the many coexistent or comorbid conditions that can occur. Any and all of the foregoing disorders may present as comorbid conditions. That is, they may coexist with one another. Major depressive disorder is a comorbid condition with anxiety conditions in over 60% of the cases (Beutler, Clarkin, & Bongar, 2000). Likewise, chemical dependence is a comorbid condition with anxiety and depressive disorders in a substantial percentage of cases (Galea et al., 2003). Moreover, personality disorders are a significant concern as comorbid conditions and tend to reduce the speed and magnitude of treatment gains (Castonguay & Beutler, 2006).

1.7   Diagnostic Procedures

Before discussing diagnostic procedures and screening/assessment, it is worth a moment to discuss the temporal aspects of early intervention care. Generally, intense emotional reactions immediately following a traumatic event are not to be considered pathological. Litz and Gray (2004) refer to this stage as the immediate impact phase in which immediate psychological and biological impacts of trauma are still present. The acute phase, as they term it, begins after the immediate impact phase and is a time in which survivors may be more apt to receive prevention interventions. For this program, we will address diagnostic procedures and interventions within three stages: (1) the acute support stage, (2) the intermediate support stage, and (3) the on-going treatment stage. Specific durations (number of days, weeks, months etc.) cannot be assigned to each stage given the uncertainties associated with mass trauma events, such as the need for repeated relocation for safety, repeated trauma (hurricane, flood, fire), and so forth, however, general temporal distinctions between stages are provided as a general guide.

Intense emotional reactions immediately following a traumatic event are not to be considered pathological

The treatment program outlined here is designed to be flexible. And, while its implementation does not depend on the establishment of a formal diagnosis, particularly in the early period following an incident event, evaluation is a central and integrated part of the process. Evaluation is embedded in the procedure throughout and is closely related to treatment. It is somewhat awkward, therefore, to separate diagnostic and evaluation procedures into a section that is separate from treatment. But, for clarity and consistency across volumes, we have done so. In this section, we will describe the evaluation procedures that are used in each of the three stages, but in actual practice, these procedures are more a part of treatment itself than a separate activity.

In the immediate period following such exposure, virtually all "survivors" will have many of the symptoms of ASD, but few of these survivors will warrant or need treatment beyond the support and resources made available informally in the first hours after an attack. Differentiation of those who will need professional care from those who will not need such treatment is not possible at this point, and selecting a diagnosis beyond describing the symptoms of acute stress is virtually impossible. The assessment concentrates on identifying those who are likely to have continuing difficulties, regardless of the diagnostic form that these may take.

Immediately following a disaster, virtually all "survivors" will have many of the symptoms of ASD

As time passes, many symptoms dissipate and change. There is no single diagnosis that is preeminent in defining one's response. Though many clinicians assume that PTSD will be the defining condition, this is not the case, and it is not until 6–8 weeks after the incident event that one can begin to identify those individuals for whom a diagnostic formulation will be helpful in planning treatment. Only at this point, is the patient's diagnosis relevant for treatment, and even then, a general rather than a specific diagnostic procedure is indicated. While a specific diagnosis will help orient treatment to fit each patient, the symptoms captured in the diagnosis are more helpful for defining how to assess and monitor change and improvement over time than to plan a truly discriminating treatment.

Only 6–8 weeks after the event can it be established for whom a diagnostic formulation will be helpful

Many scholars (e.g., Litz et al., 2002) have raised the concern that specific explorations into traumatic experiences during the immediate posttrauma period may resensitize patients to the trauma itself, and may exacerbate anxiety rather than ameliorate it. Litz et al. suggest that the failure of CISD to produce better and faster rates of recovery among some victims, relative to those in no-treatment comparison groups, may be the result of resensitization resulting from prematurely raising strong emotions about the events. Moreover, since there are both multiple kinds of response to disaster and because most people

Symptoms may be exacerbated if trauma victims are asked to discuss the trauma experience too soon

will respond positively without treatment, the assessment procedure should be less diagnostic than prognostic in focus. The basic task is to identify, as soon as possible, those who are at risk for having ongoing anxiety, depression, chemical abuse, or related conditions.

To avoid resensitizing the patient, the assessment procedure for identifying long-term risk must be as unobtrusive as possible and focused as much as possible on those factors that are known to be associated with prognosis. Moreover, because the risk of false positives (those predicted to be at risk but who are not) reduces with time, it should be implemented in stages over time, becoming increasingly honed to those who are most at risk. This staged approach permits the clinician to increasingly focus attention and the necessary resources on those who are not likely to respond resiliently. Thus, the treatment program described in this volume is presented in three stages, each of which is associated with a specific type of assessment, and each of which is embedded in a principle driven treatment protocol.

1.7.1   Introduction to Principle-Driven Treatment and Assessment

The unique aspect of the treatment program outlined in this volume is that it is based on a set of empirically derived principles of change rather than on a discrete therapeutic model. By building a treatment around empirically informed principles and using strategies that have been tested and researched in controlled research, the likelihood of treatment being demonstrably effective is increased.

The treatment program is uniquely based on a set of empirically derived principles of change rather than on a discrete therapeutic model

The principles which guide treatment were identified by a joint task force of the Society of Clinical Psychology (Division 12 of the American Psychological Association) and the North American Society for Psychotherapy Research (Castonguay & Beutler, 2006a). Twenty-five task force members and 20 affiliated authors devoted three years to reviewing extant research and extracting a list of principles of therapeutic change that met the group's criteria of efficacy. Subgroups worked on each of four problem areas: depressive spectrum disorders, anxiety disorders, chemical abuse disorders, and personality disorders. Within each problem area, they focused on each of three domains of variables: Qualities of the patient and therapist (participant variables), qualities of a beneficial relationship, and characteristics of effective treatments. In each case, they did so with an eye toward expressing relationships as "principles" that cut across theoretical models and specific techniques and focused on guiding strategies.

In the final analysis, the Joint Task Force (Castonguay & Beutler, 2006b) identified a total of 26 "common" and 35 "unique" principles. Common principles are those that cut across patient problems and disorders, while unique principles are those that appear to be relatively specific to the application of treatment to certain problems. In the current treatment, we relied on both common principles and unique principles that were specific to the treatment of anxiety disorders, depression, and chemical abuse. We have modified the principles slightly to clarify them and to make them more applicable to the experiences of mass trauma and terrorism.

Twenty-eight principles addressed patient and therapist characteristics that predicted or moderated improvement. Twenty-three of these participant-based principles addressed unique and specific processes that take place in the treatment of particular problems. However, five participant-level principles were found to be common across problem areas and were specifically focused on defining prognosis from early indicators. Thus, these participant-level principles were used to guide the assessment of patients in the early stages of treatment. The relationship-level and strategy-level principles were used to guide assessment and treatment in the later stages.

28 principles address patient and therapist characteristics

Eleven principles defined and validated the role of relationship factors in treatment, all but two of which were common to all problem areas, standing in contrast to participant-level principles. The 22 principles that defined aspects of effective treatment fell in between these extremes. Nearly an equal number of treatment principles were found to be common across disorders and unique to treating different disorders. There were 12 common and 10 unique principles related to effective treatment strategies identified by the Task Force.

11 principles address the role of relationship factors in treatment and 22 principles define aspects of effective treatment

Stage 1 Assessment

In the first stage of this program, the primary assessment task of the clinician is to begin to identify those individuals who have the highest risk of long-term problems, while eliminating from further follow up those that are most likely to recover without treatment. We seek to minimize the number of false negatives in the evaluation, as opposed to reducing false positive rates, and thus, use a procedure that multiidentifies those who may have long-term problems. Five common participant principles from the Joint Task Force all focus on identifying individuals who are either at risk or for whom a poor prognosis is indicated. Thus, they are advantageous as a backdrop by which to orient the assessment of risk in this stage. These principles are presented in Table 2, and, supplemented by specific research on victim response, are used to track those who may need further intervention in Stages 2 and 3.

As one will note, level of impairment, psychiatric history of personality disorder, a history of recurrent work and interpersonal problems, and negative

---

Table 2
Common Participant Principles Guiding Stage 1 Evaluation

Inferred Characteristics of Participants

1. Clients with a high level of impairment are less likely to benefit from therapy than those with a better level of functioning at pretreatment.
2. Clients who have been diagnosed with a personality disorder are less likely to benefit from treatment than those who do not have a personality disorder.
3. Clients who face financial and/or occupational difficulties may benefit less from treatment than those who do not.

Observed Characteristics of Participants

1. Clients who experienced significant interpersonal problems during their early development may have difficulty responding to psychotherapy.
2. Client's expectations are likely to influence treatment outcome

expectations (e.g., loss of hope) tend to identify those who are at risk and who are at risk for poor response to intervention efforts. We operationalized and refined the patterns noted in the results of the Joint Task Force using information from direct research on the survivors of 9/11/2001 over an extended period of time (e.g., Galea et al., 2002; Galea et al., 2003). This research confirms the roles of the principle-based variables and adds prior exposure to violence and trauma as poor prognostic indicators.

In the first hours and days following a terrorist attack, a variety of responders, including health care and case workers, ordinarily assist in the overall relief effort. These individuals provide psychological first aid and offer support. It is during the course of these duties, and over a period of approximately 5 days following the incident events, that these workers are asked to engage survivors in conversations sufficient to determine if they have any of five characteristics that emerge from the Joint Task Force and 9/11 reports to suggest risk:

1. Premorbid personality and major psychiatric disorder: A pre-event history of personality disorder or treatment of severe psychiatric disorder;
2. Severity of symptoms: Multiple symptoms of distress that impair current functioning and hamper reality testing;
3. Social support deficits: Inadequate social support from family or community agencies;
4. Interpersonal difficulties: A history of difficulties with people, with the law, and with authorities; and
5. Prior exposure to trauma (previous traumatization): A history of previous exposure to trauma and/or violence to a sufficient degree that the individual being assessed sought or were referred for treatment.

Evaluation is conducted using a conversational rather than a clinical manner

We initiate this evaluation as unobtrusively as possible, using a conversational rather than a clinical manner, in order to avoid both resensitization and exacerbation of the concerns that victims may have about their future. We also avoid intense discussions of the incident event itself, unless the victim seems driven to recount these events. We encourage case workers, mental health personnel, or other crisis responders who are assigned to make these first contacts, to guide the patient in a discussion of the relevant information through one or two conversations, the primary and obvious focus of which is on obtaining resources and connecting the identified survivor with social support systems and community resources.

Once one or more of these five conditions are defined as being present, the patient's name and contact information is put on a list for follow up in Stage 2. *A specific effort is made to make this list multiinclusive.* Those who are judged to have positive responses on one or more of these indicators are entered automatically into the second stage of treatment. Those among them who have a history of psychosis, taking antipsychotic medications, or who are currently hallucinating or delusional are referred for immediate psychiatric evaluation and care.

There are no formal instruments suited to this Stage 1 evaluation. While this reduces the likelihood of retraumatization, it may play into the difficulty that some clinicians have in letting anyone suffer who has experienced trauma. A clinician's general inclination is to identify anyone who is in pain as someone who is at risk. In mass trauma, this tendency over burdens the system.

We encourage the clinician to understand the reality that not all people can or should be treated and followed. We aim to reduce the pool of victims by at least 50% in this early evaluation.

Not all people can or should be treated or followed

Stage 2 Assessment

In the second stage of the intervention, which begins after the first week following the terrorist event, one can begin to assess the strength of symptoms of ASD. To a large extent, the symptoms assessed at Stage 2 are the same as those assessed in Stage 1. Indeed, if the symptoms have continued unabated, action is required in Stage 2 to help relieve the problems. To a large extent, the symptoms assessed serve as indicators of the severity of the patient's reaction and are referenced to the symptoms that characterize ASD, though even this disorder is so over shadowed with the incident event itself that its diagnosis is of limited value.

Table 3 provides a list of the criteria for ASD; patient status on these symptoms is used to evaluate severity of reaction. Evaluation of these features, as in the first stage of the treatment program, are best done quite informally in order to avoid resensitization.

Table 3
Diagnostic Criteria for ASD and PTSD

Acute Stress Disorder

A. Exposure to traumatic event
- Experienced, witnessed, or confronted with event(s) that involved actual or threatened death or serious injury, or threat to physical integrity of self or others
- The person's response involved intense fear, helplessness, or horror

B. Either while experiencing or after experiencing the distressing event, the individual has three or more of the following dissociative symptoms:
- A subjective sense of numbing, detachment, or absence of emotional responsiveness
- A reduction in awareness of his or her surroundings
- Derealization
- Depersonalization
- Dissociative amnesia

C. The traumatic event is persistently reexperienced in at least one of the following ways:
- Recurrent images
- Thoughts
- Dreams
- Illusions
- Flashback episodes
- Sense of reliving the experience
- Distress on exposure to reminders of the traumatic event

D. Marked avoidance of stimuli that arouse recollections of the trauma

E. Marked symptoms of anxiety or increased arousal

Table 3 (continued)

F. The disturbance causes clinically significant distress or impairment in social, occupational, or other important areas of functioning or impairs the individual's ability to pursue some necessary task, such as obtaining necessary assistance or mobilizing personal resources by telling family members about the traumatic experience

G. The disturbance lasts for a minimum of two days and a maximum of 4 weeks and occurs within 4 weeks of the traumatic event

The disturbance is not due to the direct physiological effects of a substance or a general medical condition, is not better accounted for by brief psychotic disorder, and is not merely an exacerbation of a preexisting Axis I or II disorder

Posttraumatic Stress Disorder

A. Exposure to traumatic event
   - Experienced, witnessed, or confronted with event(s) that involved actual or threatened death or serious injury, or threat to physical integrity of self or others
   - The person's response involved intense fear, helplessness, or horror

B. Traumatic event is reexperienced in one or more of the following ways:
   - Recurrent and intrusive distressing recollections of the event
   - Recurrent distressing dreams of the event
   - Acting or feeling as if the traumatic event were recurring
   - Intense psychological distress at exposure to internal or external cues that symbolize or resemble an aspect of the traumatic event
   - Physiological reactivity on exposure to internal or external cues that symbolize or resemble as aspect of the traumatic event

C. Persistent avoidance of stimuli associated with the trauma and numbing of general responsiveness (not present before the trauma) via three or more of the following:
   - Efforts to avoid thoughts, feelings, or conversations associated with the trauma
   - Efforts to avoid activities, places, or people that arouse recollections of the trauma
   - Inability to recall an important aspect of the trauma
   - Markedly diminished interest or participation in significant activities
   - Feeling of detachment or estrangement from others
   - Restricted range of affect
   - Sense of foreshortened future

D. Persistent symptoms of increased arousal (not present before the trauma) as indicated by two or more of the following:
   - Difficulty falling or staying asleep
   - Irritability or outbursts of anger
   - Difficulty concentrating
   - Hypervigilance
   - Exaggerated startle response

Duration of the disturbance (symptoms in Criteria B, C, and D) is more than one month

The disturbance causes clinically significant distress or impairment in social, occupational or other important areas of functioning

Table 4
Prognostic Symptoms

- Severe ASD symptoms
- High levels of physical symptoms
- Preexisting or comorbid psychopathology
- Display of high active avoidance
- Maladaptive attributions of symptoms
- Serious physical injury
- Low level of social support
- Derealization and flashbacks

Assessment of these symptoms can take several forms. For example, a semistructured interview or mini-mental state examination (Folstein, Folstein, & McHugh, 1975) may be used to assess overall functioning. This procedure is also helpful to identify the degree to which several prognostic symptoms are present (see Table 4).

Alternatively, one may find self-report measures helpful. Brewin et al. (2002) developed a brief screening instrument for PTSD symptoms that was shown to have excellent predictive ability in a study with independent samples. The instrument, the *Trauma Screening Questionnaire* (TSQ), is comprised of 10 statements that require the individual to answer yes or no to whether they have experienced the listed reactions. Brewin et al. recommend that this screening instrument should only be used when 3 or 4 weeks have elapsed after a traumatic event.

Evaluation at this stage focuses on three indicators of ASD symptoms that are frequent during the initial postevent period, but which tend to dissipate by the second week after exposure among those who do not have a continuing high risk of long-term problems with anxiety (Marmar, Weiss, & Metzler, 1997). The indicators include: (1) continuing presence of flashbacks, (2) periods of derealization, and (3) feelings of disembodiment and depersonalization. We use the following questions, extracted from the Peritraumatic Dissociative Experiences Questionnaire (Marmar et al., 1997), to identify these symptoms in an unobtrusive manner.

> **Evaluation in Stage 2 focuses on 3 indicators of ASD problems**

- Do you ever lose track of what is going on around you? That is do you ever "blank out," or feel "spaced out" and don't feel part of what is going on?
- Do you ever lose time?
- Do you ever end up doing things that you haven't actively decided to do?
- Does your sense of time ever change, when things seem to be happening in slow motion?
- Do you ever feel as though you are a spectator, watching what is happening to you as if you were an outsider?
- Do you ever feel as though you are disoriented, as though you are uncertain about where you are or what time it is?

A positive response to any of these questions raises the concern of long-term problems, and, consistent with the effort to remain over inclusive, results

Table 5
Topics of Education in Stage 2

Avoidance of thoughts, activities, places, and any other reminders
- Avoidance is another attempt to minimize the hurtful memories of what happened and prevent it from happening again

Physical arousal
- Being hyperaware of your surroundings, having trouble sleeping or concentrating, feeling restless and irritable, or having a sense of impending danger or doom
- Physical arousal is a sign that even though the trauma is over, your body is still in alert mode and prepared for the worst, ready to fight or flee
- Nightmares

Loss of Interest in Things
- Lack of interest in activities that have been enjoyable in the past
- Lethargic and uninvolved in activities or things that are usually considered to be pleasant.
- Withdrawal from social events, parties, and gatherings.

Loss of Appetite
- Loss of interest in food, unaware of being hungry, loss of weight without making an effort to do so.
- Usually sought after foods are ignored.

Worry over Little Things
- Excessive preoccupation with things that make little difference or have limited consequences,
- Distracted by minutia and becomes upset by the anticipation of eventualities that are of little significance to others.

in the identified "survivor" being listed for follow up into the third stage of treatment.

The occasion of this semistructured evaluation is also an opportunity to educate patients about some particularly difficult and predictive symptoms that they may experience. Table 5 provides definitions that are used to educate patients to be self-reflective and evaluative.

Stage 3 Assessment

Formal assessment of risk and differential treatment response can occur in Stage 3

The empirically informed principles (see Section 4) that guide the interventions in Stage 3 include those that will help tailor the intervention to both the problem and the reaction patterns of the victims. Thus, it is in the third stage of the program that the use of formal assessment procedures are warranted in order to maximize the level of reliability of the findings. At this point, both diagnostic and nondiagnostic dimensions are useful.

The decisions about differential treatment that are made in the third stage of intervention will lead us to make modifications to the strategies used in order to alter the level of therapist direction and control applied, as well as the level of treatment intensity. Following the principles of intervention framed by the Joint Task Force (described in Section 4 of this manual), we base our differential treatment decisions on an assessment of the degree of impairment and of the level of interpersonal cooperation of which the patient victim is capable. The principles that underlie and guide the current treatment program emphasize that patients who have high levels of resistance are unlikely to benefit from high levels of clinician direction and control, such as is often present in stress-management programs. Patients who do best in a stress management program are typically those who can tolerate being a follower and who are not prone to being argumentative and controlling (Beutler, Clarkin, & Bongar, 2000; Castonguay & Beutler, 2006).

The dimensions of impairment level and resistance to external control can be assessed with a variety of assessment procedures, including standardized, objective personality tests (e.g., Minnesota Multiphasic Personality Inventory 2– MMPI-2; Millon Clinical Multiaxial Inventory-III – MCMI-III), clinical interviews (e.g., Structured Clinical Interview for the DSM-IV – SCID-IV), and symptom self-reports (e.g., Symptom Checklist 90 Revised – SCL-90R; Beck Depression Inventory – BDI). Our own preference is to emphasize the use of short, self-report instruments, supplemented by clinician observations. Measures of depression, anxiety, social functioning, relationships, coping style, and general well-being are helpful to direct the future course of treatment. Beutler and colleagues (Beutler & Groth-Marnat, 2003; Harwood & Williams, 2003) have developed an assessment procedure that captures all of these dimensions, the Systematic Treatment Selection (STS) Procedure. This tool has comparable forms for patient and clinician, has demonstrated utility, and provides a platform on which clinicians can summarize their impressions and identify the most dominant problems and problems in coping. The details of this assessment procedure are presented elsewhere (Harwood & Williams, 2003).

In the STS assessment system, impairment level estimates are derived from several indicators, including the patient's diagnosis, the level of social support being received by the victim, the level of comorbidity, and the chronicity of the symptoms being presented. A standard diagnostic interview provides the initial basis for establishing a diagnosis (see Beutler & Groth-Marnat, 2003), which can be supplemented by exploring social support systems and comorbidity. The complexity and comorbidity of the problems present can be estimated by exploring the following questions:

1. Has there been more than one similar episode of the presenting problem, or of major depression?
2. Does this patient merit more than one Axis I diagnosis?
3. Has the patient had the current or another diagnosed psychiatric condition continuously for more than six months?
4. Is there a long history of recurrent problems with depression and/or social relations?

Another component of impairment, based on patient levels of social support, may also be obtained through a historical review, and by addressing the following types of questions, a positive answer to any one of which suggests poor functioning (Beutler & Harwood, 2000):

1. Does the patient lack one or more friends with whom he or she seems to share common interests?
2. Does the patient report feeling like others don't trust or respect him?
3. Does the patient lack at least one friend or family member in whom he or she can confide?

4. Does the patient feel abandoned or rejected by family and relatives?
5. Does the patient feel lonely most of the time, even when with others?
6. Is the patient not currently a member of a perceived family unit?

The second major dimension, *interpersonal sensitivity and cooperation* (sometimes called resistance), can be derived from explorations of the patient's history with authority figures (Beutler & Harwood, 2000). From this review, one can obtain information about the following factors, a preponderance of which may indicate problems with therapeutic cooperation:

1. Has trouble following the advice of those in authority
2. Is confrontive in relationships with others
3. Is critical of other's mistakes
4. Believes that others will take advantage of him or hcr
5. Is not open to new experiences
6. Is controlling in relationships
7. Is passive-aggressive
8. Fails to keep commitments to others
9. Ignores or fails to seek assistance when having trouble
10. Is distrustful and suspicious of others' motives
11. Is easily offended or hurt by others' criticisms
12. Has strong and unbendable opinions about things
13. Disregards social rules
14. Is argumentative
15. Has been told that he or she is oppositional or rebellious

Ordinarily, the clinician inspects the patient's history, asks questions to be able to assess the foregoing dimensions, and makes a reasoned judgment of whether the patient falls high or low on the two dimensions evaluated (functional impairment and interpersonal sensitivity). Once that decision is made, the clinician is ready to present the treatment recommendations to the victim/ patient and to begin to develop the treatment program

2

Theories and Models

Most manual-based treatments focus on a specific disorder. Since there is not a specific disorder associated with exposure to mass trauma and terrorism, there is not a specific model of the disorder with which to accurately contrast the current treatment. Nonetheless, we will describe several general models that have been used for trauma-related conditions. After doing so, it will be advantageous to step back and inspect the issues of empirically supported treatments from a broad perspective, with special focus on the controversies that have centered on how best to approach the task of identifying effective treatments. This will help us place the current program within an appropriate framework.

> General models for trauma-related conditions include learning/cognitive models and conservation of resources models

2.1   Learning/Cognitive Models of Posttrauma Response

Most current models of posttraumatic responding (and PTSD) combine elements of learning theory and cognitive psychology. Cognitive-behavioral theories of PTSD (e.g.., Foa et al., 1989; Keane, Zimering, & Caddell, 1985) suggest that stimuli present at time of traumatization may come, through a process of classical conditioning, to elicit conditioned emotional responses similar to those experienced during the trauma itself. If emotional experiences during trauma exposure were extremely intense (e.g., panic, freezing), aspects of these same intense responses may be elicited by trauma-related stimuli (e.g., situations, events, or "reminders"). Trauma memories that were encoded in a context of intense anxiety or other traumatic emotional arousal may be characterized by poor elaboration and contextualization; for example they may be remembered mainly as sensory impressions, disconnected from memory of other parts of the experience, and not organized in a coherent narrative account of what happened. Such memories may be easily and involuntarily triggered by a wide range of reminders, and feel as if they are happening right now. The Ehlers and Clark (2000) cognitive model of PTSD asserts that PTSD results when individuals process their traumatic experience in ways that serve to maintain a sense of serious, ongoing current threat. When traumatic memories have the characteristics noted above, this may contribute to a sense of continuing threat.

> PTSD results when individuals process their traumatic experiences in ways that serve to maintain their sense of serious, ongoing current threat

Foa (1997) outlined psychological processes related to natural recovery following exposure to a trauma. Recovery from a traumatic experience is associated with emotional engagement with a traumatic memory (as opposed to avoidance of reminders, emotional withdrawal, and dissociation), organization and articulation of the memory, and maintenance of a balanced view about the dangerousness of the world and competency of the self. Beliefs that "the world is completely dangerous" and "I am totally incompetent" are held to be two primary dysfunctional cognitions that mediate development of PTSD (Foa & Rothbaum, 1998). Such a focus on appraisal or personal meaning of the trauma is similarly emphasized by Ehlers and Clark (2000): individuals who view their experience as a time-limited one that does not have great implications for the future are expected to be more likely to recover well than those who have excessively negative appraisals. Individuals who, after trauma, view the world as a very dangerous place, make negative judgments about themselves, have negative interpretations about their symptoms or the reactions of other people, or conclude that their lives have been permanently worsened will be more likely to develop problems. Such negative trauma-related beliefs may, like some kinds of traumatic memories, maintain acute stress reactions by invoking threatening expectations for the future.

Recovery requires emotional engagement with a traumatic memory

A theme of personal competence is also evident in the social cognitive theory of posttraumatic recovery (Benight & Bandura, 2003), which highlights the role of perceived self-efficacy as a determinant of posttrauma functioning. Perceived self-efficacy is defined as "perceived capability to manage one's personal functioning and the myriad environmental demands of the aftermath occasioned by a traumatic event" (Benight & Bandura, 2003, p. 1129). Importantly, a sense of coping efficacy is one determinant of coping actions. Individuals with high coping self-efficacy are more likely to mobilize and sustain coping efforts. Following the Oklahoma City terrorist bombing, perceptions of self-efficacy to manage occupation, emotional life, and intrusive thoughts and dreams predicted which individuals were in workplaces adjacent to the bombing

In addition to perceived ability to cope, actual choice of coping actions may also affect outcomes of exposure to traumatic events. Most theories stress, in particular, that extreme avoidance coping may operate to prevent recovery by reducing opportunities for change in negative appraisals or processing of the traumatic memory (Ehlers & Clark, 2000; Foa & Rothbaum, 1998), or extinction of conditioned emotional responses (Zimering & Caddell, 1985). Key avoidance behaviors that may interfere with recovery if they become frequent or pervasive include alcohol and drug use, social withdrawal, and physical isolation.

2.2   Conservation of Resources Model

Conservation of resources theory (Hobfall, 1989; Hobfoll, Dunahoo, & Monnier, 1995) predicts that distress and other negative outcomes of traumatization will be related to the extent to which individuals are able to maintain personally-significant resources. According to this model, resources are broadly defined to include object resources (possessions with functional or status value), condition resources (including a variety of social roles), personal characteristic resources (self and world views), and energy resources (e.g., time, money, and information). This model is important in going beyond a focus on intrapersonal variables to include external factors that affect recovery. For example, loss of material resources, such as food, clothing, money, or transportation, may be problematic by imposing ongoing adversity (maintaining an ongoing sense of threat), interfering with many aspects of daily functioning (Hobfall et al., 2003), and limited access to potential solutions to problems. Some research has indicated that amount of resource loss is a significant predictor of postdisaster distress (e.g., Freedy, Shaw, Jarrell, & Masters, 1992; Sattler, Preston, Kaiser, Olivera, Valdez, & Schlueter, 2002). Resource loss may be especially important following events involving mass violence, which may result in extensive loss of resources.

> **Loss of personal resources is related to the severity of distress**

2.3 Identifying Research-Based Treatment Methods

The last decade has seen increasing emphasis on research-based practice and the importance of validating the effects of treatments through systematic research. Two major movements have defined this effort to incorporate research-based knowledge into practice within the arena of psychotherapy. These include treatment-centered and relationship-centered approaches. The first of these has paralleled contemporary practices in the medical field and has sought to identify and empirically validate the efficacy of formal treatment procedures and models that are assumed to be effective for specific diagnostic conditions. This approach (e.g., Nathan & Gorman, 2003) relies on defining the nature of treatments in a reliable way and then pitting one treatment against another, or against a no-treatment condition, on a population of individuals with a given disorder or diagnosis, in order to establish the efficacy of the treatment. This approach relies on the use of treatment manuals to ensure the fidelity and replicability of the intervention, the identification of group of like-diagnosed patients who are willing to be randomly assigned to a treatment and no-treatment condition, and systematic assessment of long and short outcomes. The question addressed by these methods is that of efficacy, i.e., "Does this treatment work?" Occasionally, the question is expanded to address the issue of which of two or more treatments is most efficacious.

> **APA and NASPR Joint Task Force on "Empirically Supported Principles of Treatment that Work aims to address the limits of other approaches**

The limitations of this treatment-centered viewpoint include the following:
- It places the focus of validation on the validity of the theories of treatment.
- Thus, many predictors and correlates of change, which are not integral parts of the theory or model of change, are ignored.
- It relies on the use of structured treatment manuals and diagnostic groupings of patients to control the effects of therapist judgment, patient factors, and relationship factors. Thus, these qualities are not assessed, except occasionally after the fact, as to their role in therapeutic success. In treating the effects of terrorism, for example, this may represent a particular problem because there is no single or specific patient diagnosis associated with exposure to this type of trauma. Moreover, manuals may not have the degree of flexibility required to deal with a rapidly changing and very heterogeneous population of survivors. Likewise,

controlling for rather than understanding the importance of therapist judgment and skill is unlikely to enhance the field.
- It emphasizes the use of randomized controls and true experiments to determine the effectiveness of treatment. Thus, it ignores the role of factors that cannot be randomized, such as many patient demographics, expectations, preferences, social environments, and nondiagnostic personality factors.

The task of acquiring skill in a sufficient number of empirically supported manuals to be practical is not very feasible

To further complicate the definition of treatments that can be considered empirically supported, there are no simple sets of criteria by which to evaluate these treatments and the task of acquiring skill in a sufficient range of manuals to be practical is not very feasible. There are at least 11 lists of empirically supported treatments, often overlapping but different in nature (Beutler et al., 2005; Chambless & Ollendick, 2001). In these various lists, there are over 150 different treatment models and manuals that are considered empirically supported. Each of these manuals requires 1–2 years to master and achieve satisfactory compliance and fidelity. Moreover, even this large number of manuals only address the treatment of 51 of the 397 disorders in DSM-IV. And, finally, as a capstone, the evidence that the use of manuals improves the effectiveness of treatment, vis-à-vis therapy as usual, is weak (Norcorss, Beutler, & Levant, 2006).

The relationship-centered approach to validating treatments (Norcross, 2002) was developed as an alternative to the treatment-centered approach typically used. It seeks to identify characteristics of patients, therapists, and relationships that are most predictive of change. This approach to validation of treatment focuses on qualities and variables that enhance the therapeutic bond and relationship and that tend to be ignored in theoretical models.

Relationship-centered approaches have sought to address the failure to find some approaches that are superior to others

Relationship-centered approaches to identifying what makes treatment successful have sought to address the failure of treatment-centered methods to decisively identify treatments that are superior to others. But, they, too, have limitations and weaknesses:
- By focusing on factors that contribute to the therapeutic relationship over the role of specific therapeutic models, they often ignore the possibility that there are factors, in addition to relationship qualities, that may carry weight in effecting change. In particular, they only minimally address how the roles of relationship factors might vary in different treatment models and with different therapists. Interactions among patients, therapists, and treatments are not adequately addressed.
- Likewise, though importantly emphasizing nondiagnostic participant qualities over diagnostic compliance, these approaches may underestimate the role of the nature of the problem in determining how interventions are perceived and operate. That is, they may ignore the ways that problems differ and affect individuals as well as how mediating factors may operate, or how and interactions among treatments, participants, and relationship factors might affect outcomes.
- These approaches rely on quasi-experimental research designs and meta-analyses to establish treatment factors. These procedures are helpful, but have difficulty determining causal relationships between targeted contributors to change and the change itself.

In response to the short comings that have become recognized in each of these two mainline approaches, the Society of Clinical Psychology (Division 12 of APA) and the North American Society for Psychotherapy Research (NASPR) convened a Joint Task Force on defining "Empirically Supported Principles of Treatment that Work" (Castonguay & Beutler, 2006). This Task Force was commissioned to (1) review all relevant literature on three general domains of variables: participant (patient & therapist), treatment, and relationship factors that contribute to change; 2) separate the findings to reflect four major problem areas (depression, anxiety, personality disorders, and chemical abuse), and (3) extract from each body of research a summarizing set of principles that define empirically-consistent guides for clinicians working in these areas. This approach was designed to transform the various efforts to define empirical validation into a set of integrative and research-informed principles that identify both the status of current research knowledge and express this knowledge in a way that can help the clinician organize and follow a treatment plan, cutting across theoretical models.

The Joint Task Force transformed the results of empirical validation into a set of research-informed principles

3

Diagnosis and Treatment Indications: Applying Research-Based Principles

The treatment of survivors takes place within 3 temporally-based and principle-driven stages of care, with assessment at each stage

The treatment of survivors of mass trauma and terrorism takes place within three stages. As noted earlier, the population of focus is defined, in the earliest stage, by their reported exposure to the event, rather than by their compliance to a set of diagnostic criteria. Everyone who is either referred for or seeks assistance is provided with the first level of intervention, which is integrated with the Stage 1 evaluations that have been described previously.

In the second stage of treatment, the population treated is comprised of those who were assessed as being at risk in Stage 1 assessment. This includes all of those seen in the first stage who have revealed (1) a pre-event history of personality disorder or treatment of severe psychiatric disorder; (2) multiple symptoms of distress that impair current functioning and hamper reality testing; (3) a failure of available sources of social support from family or community agencies; (4) a history of interpersonal difficulties; and (5) previous exposure to earlier traumatic events.

Table 6
Principles Guiding Stage 2 of Intervention

Quality of the therapeutic relationship

1. Therapy is likely to be beneficial if a strong working alliance is established and maintained during the course of treatment.
2. Clients are likely to benefit from group therapy if a strong level of group cohesion is developed and maintained during therapy.
3. Therapists should attempt to facilitate a high degree of collaboration with clients during therapy

Interpersonal skills of the therapist

1. Therapists should relate to their clients in an empathic way.
2. When adopted by therapists, an attitude of caring, warmth, and acceptance is likely to be helpful in facilitating therapeutic change.
3. Therapists are likely to facilitate change when adopting an attitude of congruence or authenticity.

Clinical skills of the therapist

1. Therapists should use relational interpretations quite sparingly.
2. When relational interpretations are used, they are likely to facilitate improvement if they are accurate.
3. Therapists can resolve ruptures to the alliance by addressing such ruptures in an empathic and flexible way

The Joint Task Force principles that guide treatment at this stage are common to a variety of disorders and symptoms and emphasize general influences of the therapeutic relationship on change. Table 6 identifies these principles.

The application of these principles will vary somewhat from clinician to clinician, based in part upon the theoretical model from which they were drawn and the experiences that have preceded their use. Scientific data have not identified one superior theoretical model through which to apply these principles. Thus, one remains reliant on the clinician's ability, skill, and judgment to define how a given patient may be best approached and through what procedures the principle will be effectively utilized.

Treatment is offered in Stage 3 if (1) the patient warrants an Axis I diagnosis and (2) there is reasonable indication that this diagnosis is secondary to the exposure to mass terrorist trauma. It is important to note that in our early assessment, we would ordinarily identify individuals with a major premorbid condition and send them directly to treatment, circumventing Stages 2 and 3 of this program. If, in the course of evaluating individuals at Stage 2, we find some individuals whom we failed to identify as needing immediate treatment in Stage 1, by virtue of having a preexisting or exacerbated psychiatric disorder, they would also be directly referred for psychiatric evaluation and treatment.

Systematic diagnosis only occurs in the third stage of treatment. At this point, a general evaluation procedure is used to define the nature of the problem and the diagnoses. Rather than seeking a group with a specific diagnosis, however, the diagnostic information is used to tailor the treatment and to evaluate changes in symptom patterns over time.

The Joint Task Force principles of treatment (Castonguay & Beutler, 2006a) that guide treatment in the third stage of the intervention are of two types. Common principles are those that are generalizable across a variety of conditions. These common principles are designed to guide applications of all interventions at this stage. In addition, unique principles are those that guide treatment within specific types of problems. These unique principles offer the option for fine tuning and tailoring the intervention to fit different patients. The common principles are presented in Table 7.

Unique principles offer the opportunity of tailoring the intervention to different patients

It will be noted that in this stage, the principles begin to emphasize the use of traditional psychotherapeutic strategies for exploring cognitions, behaviors, and feelings. Moreover, some of the principles begin to emphasize differential applications of different interventions. Thus, regardless of the patient's particular diagnosis, intensifying treatment is indicated if the patient has severe problems or Axis II problems (Principle 2) and emotionally focused exposure is suggested (Principles 9 & 10) if the patient has exceedingly high and intolerable levels of anxiety. Alterations in the format of therapy are also suggested, across diagnostic conditions, to include multiperson therapy for assisting with interpersonal problems, and supportive structure is indicated to help the patient navigate the difficult waters of recovery.

Specific or unique principles also focus on tailoring the treatment to particular problems. The Joint Task Force unique principles emphasize three particular variations in treatment, one that adds to the already present suggestion that one may alter the intensity (frequency and type of treatments offered), a second that adjusts the balance of using internally focused or behaviorally

Table 7
Common Principles for Applying Stage 3 Treatment

Therapeutic stance and general interpersonal style

1. Positive change is likely if the therapist provides a structured treatment and remains focused in the application of his or her interventions.
2. Therapists should be able to skillfully use nondirective or self-directive as well as directive interventions.

Framework of intervention

3. Time-limited therapy can be beneficial.
4. Therapeutic change may be facilitated by, or even require, intense therapy if a personality disorder or severe problem is present.

Interpersonal/systemic versus intrapersonal/individual procedures

5. Therapist may be more effective if he/she does not restrict him/herself to individual procedures: Being with others during treatment can be beneficial for some clients.
6. Effective therapy may require therapists to address intrapersonal aspects of the client's functioning.
7. Therapy outcome is likely to be enhanced if therapy addresses interpersonal issues related to clinical problems.

Thematic/insight-oriented versus symptom/skill building procedures

8. Therapy is likely to be beneficial if therapist facilitates change in clients' cognitions.
9. The client is likely to benefit from therapy if therapist helps him/her modify maladaptive behavioral, emotional, or physiological responses.
10. Facilitating client self exploration can be helpful

Abreactive versus emotionally supportive procedures

11. Therapeutic change is likely if the therapist helps clients accept, tolerate, and at times, fully experience their emotions.
12. Interventions aimed at controlling emotions can be helpful

focused procedures to adapt to patient internalizing and externalizing coping styles, and a third which emphasizes the value of varying the level of therapist control to accommodate resistance. The selection of these modifications are made with reference to both the major symptoms (anxiety, depression, chemical abuse) and the associated Joint Task Force principles that guide specific intervention strategies (Beutler, Clarkin, & Bongar, 2000; Castonguay & Beutler, 2006). Table 8 summarizes these unique principles, separately for anxiety and depressed patients.

It should be noted that the Joint Task Force identified four unique principles that can be applied to chemical abuse problems, as well. While initially defined for the treatment of smoking, we believe that they may be equally valid for treating other forms of chemical abuse and dependency as well. Thus, they are presented in Table 9, rephrased slightly to reflect the treatment of patients whose constellation of symptoms include drug dependency and abuse.

Observing the unique principles applied to treating victims who present with substantial amounts of anxiety, depression, and chemical abuse, one may first wonder at the disparity between the number of unique principles guiding

Table 8
Unique Principles for Guiding Stage 3 Change

Anxiety Symptoms

1. Psychotherapy for anxiety is less likely to be successful if the client has low internal attributions of control or high negative self-attribution. Thus, rigid externalizing or internalizing coping styles are negative prognostic indicators.
2. Providing feedback to the client is beneficial.

Depressive Symptoms

1. Age is a negative predictor of a patient's response to general psychotherapy.
2. Patients representing underserved ethnic or racial group achieve fewer benefits than Anglo-American groups from conventional psychotherapy.
3. If patients and therapists come from the same or similar racial/ethnic backgrounds, drop out rates are positively affected and improvement is enhanced.
4. The most effective treatments are likely to be those that do not induce patient resistance.
5. In dealing with the resistant patient, the therapist's use of directive therapeutic interventions should be planned to inversely correspond with the patient's manifest level of resistant traits and states.
6. Patients with high levels of initial impairment respond better when they are offered long-term, intensive treatment, than when they receive nonintensive and brief treatments, regardless of the particular model and type of treatment assigned. Patients with low impairment seem to do equally well in high and low intensive treatments.
7. Patients whose personalities are characterized by impulsivity, social gregariousness, and external blame for problems, benefit more from direct behavioral change and symptom reduction efforts, including building new skills, and managing impulses, than they do from procedures that are designed to facilitate insight and self-awareness.
8. Patients whose personalities are characterized by low levels of impulsivity, indecisiveness, self-inspection, and over control, tend to benefit more from procedures that foster self-understanding, insight, interpersonal attachments, and self-esteem, than they do from procedures that aim at directly altering symptoms and building new social skills.
9. If psychotherapists are open, informed, and tolerant of various religious views, treatment effects are likely to be enhanced.
10. If patients have a preference for religiously oriented psychotherapy, treatment benefit is enhanced if therapists accommodate this preference.
11. A secure attachment pattern in the therapist appears to facilitate the treatment process.
12. Benefit may be enhanced when the interventions selected are responsive to and consistent with the patient's level of problem assimilation.
13. When working with depressed clients, therapists' use of self-disclosure is likely to be helpful. This may especially be the case for reassuring and supportive self-disclosures, as opposed to challenging self-disclosures.

the treatment of depression, compared to those addressing chemical abuse and anxiety. This may be partially an artifact, however, and reflective of the large body of research on specific treatments for depression, compared to anxiety disorders.

Additionally, one may note that the principles related to treating anxiety emphasize the role of patient coping style, with the suggestion that internalizing or self-directed patients are better prognostic risks than those who are

Table 9
Unique Principles Guiding the Treatment of Chemical Abuse Disorders

1. Therapists with vs. without a history of substance use disorder appear to be equally effective in treating alcohol or illicit drug abuse.

2. High-medical-risk users will be especially receptive to individual counseling for drug use cessation only if drug abuse and use is plausibly contributing to their risk status.

3. Although the evidence is not entirely consistent, cognitive behavior therapy may be differentially effective with depressed drug users relative to comparison conditions. This prescriptive effect may apply especially to those drug abusing victims with chronic, recurrent depression.

4. Identify other social service or medical care needs and arrange for attention to these needs.

not self-reflective (e.g., externalizing patients). In either case, the positive and ameliorating role of feedback is emphasized for treating anxious patients, perhaps reflecting the value of calming reassurance and structuring.

This latter theme is expanded in the principles that guide the treatment of depressed victims. Depression Principles 7 and 8, however, elaborate on the added value of specifically adjusting the degree to which the therapist guides the victim to focus on facilitating insight and becoming aware of internal experience, compared to specifically teaching coping skills and behavioral controls, as a function of how one comes to cope with the traumatic event. Those who question themselves and become self-reflective and emotionally isolated tend to be candidates for interventions that facilitate insight, while those who are impulsive and avoidant are candidates for behavioral skills training.

Treatment of depression focuses on the added value of adjusting the degree to which the therapist guides the victim through insight or behavior change

In a similar way, Depression Principle 6 reinforces the common principles that we previously described by emphasizing the need to take special care with victims who present with especially severe and impairing problems. It is suggested that treatment intensity be adapted to the victim's level of impairment, with more intensive interventions being applied to more impaired individuals. Increasing the length, frequency, and variety of interventions often will support this principle.

Treatment intensity should be adapted to the patient's level of impairment

One also notes that the guiding principles for treating depressed victims emphasize both prognostic and differential applications of treatment. One should remain aware of the need to be sensitive to demographic differences and values, especially age, ethnic background, and religion. Flexibility and acceptance of diversity are positive characteristics to foster in a therapist who works with diverse client/victims.

One also notes that it is in the treatment of victims with significant levels of dysphoria and depression, that the fit of treatment is most clearly specified with respect to adapting treatment to patient coping style, problem severity, and resistance. Principle 5 emphasizes the need to counter balance the victim's level of resistance with the therapist's level of directiveness and control. Victimized individuals are likely to be very sensitive to loss of personal control over their lives and thus, listening and facilitating rather than guiding and controlling is indicated when this is noted.

A series of studies on resistance among chemical abusing patients (Karno & Longabaugh, 2003, 2004, 2005), as well as three from our own research group (Beutler, Clarkin, & Bongar, 2000; Beutler, Moliero, Malik et al., 2003; Karno, Beutler, & Harwood, 2002) have found patient resistance to be a consistent moderator of the effectiveness of therapist directiveness among chemical abusing patients, in the same way it is identified in depression. Thus, in the current program, we apply principles that guide the degree of therapist directiveness applied to alter chemical abuse, in the same way as we do to those victims who are characterized by depression and dysphoria. The principles of effective change suggest that all of the active procedures that we will describe in subsequent sections should be monitored closely by the clinician in order to avoid activating victim resistance. As resistance is observed, the clinician is advised to back off and assume a supportive stance.

Patient resistance should be monitored

To facilitate adapting interventions to fit victim coping styles, we have differentiated, in the following sections, among procedures that address internal experience and those that address behavioral control and change. One set of interventions emphasize prolonged exposure and reliving of the traumatic events. This focus in treatment invokes discussion and visualization of the trauma and discussions of its impact, memories, and reworking of relationships with lost loved ones and colleagues. It is likely to be maximally effective among patients who have clinically depressed affect and mood and who tend to rely on internalizing coping strategies. Internalizing coping styles are indicated by a preference for coping through emotional isolation, self-blame, rumination, and stress-related physical symptoms.

Exposure is more effective with clinically depressed patients

A second group of interventions that are described in the following sections emphasize the development of new action-oriented coping skills, including identifying maladaptive cognitions and behaviors, learning socially adaptive skills for making and maintaining social relationships, and establishing moderated emotional control. These procedures may be most effective among victims who are externally focused and who tend to act out, avoid issues, or otherwise to use externalizing coping strategies to deal with change. Externalizing patients tend to blame others, use excuses, directly avoid confrontation, emphasize denial and minimization of one's own social roles, and become aggressive when confronted.

Action-oriented coping skills training is most effective with externally focused patients

Coping style can be assessed in many different ways (Beutler et al., 2002; Beutler & Moos, 2004). For treatment planning, it represents the degree to which one prefers one of the styles over the other and is assessed as a ratio between externalizing and internalizing styles. Measurement of these tendencies can be obtained in a variety of ways, but the two most used procedures are the use of the Minnesota Multiphasic Personality Inventory (MMPI) and the Systematic Treatment Selection (STS) procedure (Beutler & Groth-Marnat, 2003). In both instances, scales representing internalizing tendencies are weighed against those suggesting externalizing traits. A balance in favor of one or the other is used to nurture the discussions with patients about which of the two treatments to encourage. These measures are then used, along with the estimates of impairment and interpersonal sensitivity previously described, in developing tailored treatment plans.

4

Treatment: Applying the 3-Stage Model of Principle-Driven Treatment for Early Intervention Following Mass Casualty Events

The current treatment program is designed to emphasize and build on both the treatment-centered and the relationship-centered approaches, but does so within the framework of the previously described empirically-informed principles of therapeutic change. Each stage of the three-stage treatment model is designed to employ procedures whose effectiveness has been tested in research programs, and to do so within the framework of the research-informed principles developed by the APA Division 12/NASPR Task Force. In this section, we will describe exemplary, research-based interventions that can be used as means of both applying the principles and expanding the targets to be influenced. It should be understood, that these interventions are examples, not recipes, and simply add another layer of empirically-supported actions to the research-informed principles that guide treatment. Readers may need to refer back to the principles that we have presented in the assessment sections in order to keep the relationship between principles and techniques clear.

In the first two treatment stages, you will recall, the principles on which treatment is based are common to various problem types, reflecting the wide variation of response that individuals are likely to experience in response to mass terrorism. The principles that guide the first stage of treatment are prognostic and direct us to identify victims who are likely to have continuing problems. We follow these victims into Stage 2 of the treatment, and perhaps into Stage 3.

In Stage 2, treatment principles reflect the healing forces that are present in a therapeutic relationship. These principles, too, are common to a variety of problems and are common to a variety of interventions. As the treatment evolves to the third stages, the guiding principles are more specific to the type of problem observed and the treatment, too, begins to be more specific in the use of techniques to address the stress-induced problems of anxiety, depression, and chemical abuse, the three largest clusters of problems observed in the postterrorism survivor. Within these symptom clusters, we also begin to adapt and tailor the treatment to address three other dimensions: (1) functional impairment, (2) coping style, and (3) interpersonal sensitivity or resistance.

There are many literary sources available to the interested reader outlining current topics in early intervention for trauma. It is not within the scope of this book to provide historical background on early intervention or to deeply address the challenges associated with current intervention practices.

Rather, the following approach is presented in a manner intended to offer the reader alternatives to add to their "tool box" of early intervention techniques. Additionally, to address the detailed "how-to's" for each intervention, technique or treatment would require a library of resources. Therefore, this book is intended for licensed mental health professionals and assumes that if the practitioner is unfamiliar with proposed techniques, appropriate instruction will be sought prior to provision of such care.

As emergency medical and mental health personnel must be armed with skill in a variety of approaches to heal the wounds resulting from traumatic events in a wide array of environments, they must also arm themselves with adaptability and flexibility. Disaster settings, whether on scene, at a nearby hospital, or in a shelter, are unpredictable. Therefore, it would be near impossible to shape a "how-to" manual that covers all potential treatments for all potential sufferings. Disaster mental health care is not an exact science and can be as much an art as it is a practice. Currently, researchers are actively trying to determine which interventions are best suited as early interventions and which are not. The following intervention program is derived from such ongoing attempts and it is important to note that the program, in its entirety, has not been tested with survivors of mass casualty incidents. Instead, it is comprised of techniques being used by a variety of professionals in a variety of settings and is intended to provide practitioners with an additional set of guidelines and techniques that may assist them in their duties until there are more conclusive research findings.

Disaster mental health is as much of an art as a practice

Not all interventions are appropriate under all circumstances, and not all circumstances even require interventions in the classic sense. Uncertainty is a fundamental component of mass trauma, and especially of terrorism, and it affects not only the survivors, but the helpers as well. So, how can such things be addressed? There is no simple answer, however, having an array of tools with which to offer your services may arguably result in a higher likelihood of being prepared for the job at hand when faced with the potential for the vastly wide ranging situations and circumstances of disaster. The art comes in knowing which tool to apply at what time and where. Science has not yet offered us the laws of disaster mental health care; thus the following sequential intervention model provides practitioners with principles that will assist them in determining their own answers to these questions.

4.1   Methods of Treatment

4.1.1   Stage 1: Acute Support

Description
Though a primary goal of postevent care is the prevention of future psychopathology, there is currently little evidence that any early posttrauma intervention can accomplish this goal (Litz, Gray, Bryant, & Adler, 2002). The goals of the acute support stage include reducing distress, improving understanding of reactions, reducing problematic coping (e.g., alcohol use), and increasing awareness of when and how to access additional services.

The main goal in the immediate aftermath of disaster is support not clinical treatment

The National Institute for Clinical Excellence (NICE, 2005) maintains that "where symptoms are mild and have been present for less than four weeks after the trauma, watchful waiting, as a way of managing the difficulties presented by people with PTSD, should be considered. A follow-up contact should be arranged within one month" (p. 4). Recognizing that many individuals will suffer from stress reactions, but that these are likely to diminish over time for most, the practitioner may offer significant assistance to the survivor by providing information, practical help, and support to enhance the individual's ability to cope with the traumatic event.

The aim of assistance in the acute stage is to enhance the individual's ability to cope with the traumatic event

Acute support, as described here, may be provided by any mental health responder, and many aspects may also be performed by other emergency responders and volunteers with appropriate training. While it is by definition provided immediately following an event, the principles may also be applied at other times. Should survivors be exposed to repeating traumatic circumstances, acute support may be appropriate for an extended period of time. Generally, acute support is conceptualized as suitable from the first minutes of a disaster up to several days postdisaster.

Acute support can be provided in a diverse range of settings including the disaster scene, shelters, hospitals, and homes. It can be used by itself, but is intended to be implemented as part of a set of integrated components of care. Acute support is provided on an individual basis and does not require more than one session with the survivor. It is designed to be applied in a flexible, principle-driven manner so that the practitioner can tailor the strategy for the individual. The actions are not time consuming and allow the practitioner to make contact with many individuals over a relatively short period of time, often necessary in mass casualty situations. The principles are reasonably simple and can be taught quickly and efficiently to new disaster mental health care workers. Information gathered from contacts with survivors can be used in triaging survivors and making initial referrals for assessment or ongoing care.

The provider may choose to simply provide support to help the survivor cope with the traumatic event

Preventing the development of future psychopathology may be of utmost importance to many practitioners, however, in recognizing that most individuals will suffer from stress reactions that are likely to diminish over time, the practitioner may chose to assist the survivor by simply providing support to enhance the individual's ability to cope with the traumatic event.

We have pointed out that the guiding principles extracted from the Joint Task Force of the APA Division 12 and NASPR are general and emphasize the characteristics of people who will respond best to intervention and those whose adaptation will be most problematic. Applying these principles within the context of the more specific tasks associated with the acute support stage of treatment will assist you in determining what activities may be most appropriate for a given survivor.

The tasks of the first treatment stage are (1) to identify victims who are at substantial risk of ongoing problems, and (2) to provide assistance in addressing real, day-to-day needs. The first of these tasks is embodied in the assessment previously discussed. Providing direct care through psychological first aid provides the mechanism through which the prognostic information will be obtained and is the most direct kind of assistance that can be given to victims.

The phrase *psychological first aid* (PFA) has come to include a variety of techniques over the years, including critical incident stress debriefing

(CISD). Recently, however, the phrase has been shaped to refer to a more specific manualized set of techniques (not including CISD) by the National Children's Traumatic Stress Network (NCTSN) and the National Center for Post Traumatic Stress Disorder (NCPTSD). This guide, *Psychological First Aid: Field Operations Guide,* was released in September, 2005, shortly following the events of Hurricane Katrina and served a wide variety of professionals responding to this disaster.

The first stage of this intervention program shares many of the techniques outlined in the *Psychological First Aid: Field Operations Guide.* Though not functioning as a therapeutic or preventative intervention (Litz et al., 2002), acute support has been included in this intervention program for years due to its effectiveness and efficiency in assisting survivors in the field with regard to basic needs and coping.

The first stage includes many of the techniques of PFA

Acute support is comprised of guidelines, tools, and principles. Guidelines are intended to provide the practitioner with a basic approach to care at this stage posttrauma. Tools are ways the practitioner may be able to assist survivors. Principles provide the practitioner with information that can help them chose what service to offer particular survivors. Acute support may be provided by any level of mental health care provider, and some aspects may also be performed by other emergency responders and volunteers with appropriate training. Typically, acute support is provided immediately following the terrorist event. The duration of aptness for this technique is dictated by the disaster. Should survivors be exposed to repeating traumatic circumstances, this level of care may be appropriate for an extended period of time. Generally, acute support is conceptualized as suitable from immediately postdisaster up to 5 days postdisaster.

In addition to providing survivors with pragmatic and sensible assistance, the benefits of acute support are manifold. To start, care in this stage can be provided in a diverse range of settings ranging from the disaster scene to shelters to hospitals to homes. It can be used by itself or as part of a sequential treatment program. Acute support is provided on an individual basis and does not require more than one session with the survivor. The philosophy of acute support (assisting with basic needs and coping ability) allows for the use of techniques in a flexible manner so that the practitioner can tailor the strategy for the individual. The techniques are not time consuming and allow the practitioner to make contact with many individuals over a relatively short period of time, thus increasing the number of individuals served. The techniques are reasonably simple and can be taught quickly and efficiently to new disaster mental health care workers. Additionally, information gathered from contacts with survivors can be used in triaging and making initial referrals or assessment for ongoing care.

The benefits of providing acute support are manifold

The main tenets of acute support include assisting with basic physical needs, quickly cultivating rapport in a caring, compassionate, and nonthreatening manner, encouraging social contact and support, dedication to shaping your approach based on the needs of the survivor, gathering information and providing information that may assist the survivor, and promoting the use of positive coping skills.

It is imperative that the ways that we help victims of crisis reflect the best scientific knowledge available. However, the nature of science means that

From scientific research we have learned that many of the things that should have been helpful were harmful

what we know and what we can recommend is always changing. The way that scientific information accumulates means that we are likely to find out more quickly when something doesn't work than when it does. Thus, from scientific research, we have learned that many of the things that we initially believed *should* have been helpful are ineffective and some are even harmful. At the same time, we are finding that many of the common sense procedures and fundamental ways of providing assistance are proving to be surprisingly helpful to people in crisis.

Despite the extensive instruction that is frequently offered and the "treatments" that are accepted as if their use represents factual and scientifically derived knowledge, actual scientifically supported and generated knowledge about what is best to do in the immediate wake of trauma is quite limited. There are, however, some general guidelines that can be derived from what research studies have been reported, and we have attempted below to digest these into a straightforward list of basic "do's" and "don'ts" for the clinician who is seeking to assist victims and rescuers in the first days following a major community crisis. Supplementing these "do's" and "don'ts" are additional common-sense based guidelines the practitioner may also want to consider. Note that these guidelines are applicable for both acute support and intermediate support stages of this intervention program.

Things to Do

Make sure your role is clearly understood and the client has given permission for you to assist

- Remember that effective response comes not from your role as a healer, but rather from your role as one who provides comfort, direct support, and useful information. You are most effective as a source of accurate information, immediate guidance, and direct assistance with the needs and demands of the present. To help reduce the immediate stress of losing one's home, it will be far more effective to assist the survivor in locating shelter than to listen empathically to the feelings of helplessness that loss entails.
- Establish a working relationship with the client. Make sure that your role is understood and that the client has given permission for you to assist. Declare very clearly your identity, credentials, and relationships to other organizations (Red Cross, employer of rescue personnel, or any other relevant entities), and establish the objectives for the encounter. Do not proceed unless the individual is willing to accept your help.
- Provide information and guidance at very practical levels. Arm yourself with as much information as you can garner, and communicate it clearly and systematically to those you encounter. Update your information regularly, using only fully authoritative sources (i.e., don't be a vehicle for transmitting rumor and misinformation). Don't provide information that is not accurate.
- Ensure that physical and safety needs (medical, shelter, food, etc.) are provided before addressing the emotional impacts of the trauma. Keep the initial focus on meeting basic needs and preserving stamina.
- Emphasize the survivor's strengths rather than weaknesses or deficits. Provide reassurance and maintain a sense of calm. If handouts or written information are used, *these materials should be carefully structured to promote expectations of resilience and recovery*, rather than providing "laundry lists" of pitfalls and symptoms.

- Direct survivors and rescuers to community resources that will provide direct and continuing support (family, community, faith-based organizations, etc.).
- It is very helpful in later contacts to have met and supported survivors in the acute response stage. Having initially received immediate and pragmatic assistance increases the chances that survivors will engage with a helper offering additional counseling services.
- Help rescuers and other responders establish and maintain boundaries, have realistic expectations, pace their efforts, and manage stress during protracted helping periods. (This includes you too.)
- Work with companions whenever possible, and let them help you maintain perspective and objectivity.

Direct survivors to community services that will provide continuing and direct support

Things to Avoid
- Debriefing in the immediate aftermath of trauma – by its many labels (PD, CISD, MSD) – has not been shown to be effective in preventing later difficulties.
- Don't push survivors to discuss or do something that they are reluctant to do. The majority of those who are exposed to even severe trauma will not develop PTSD and will recover through their own resources and in their own time. Thus, it is important to respect the natural recovery process and to avoid presuming that someone needs professional mental health assistance. As much as possible, let people set their own pace, talk about things that are important to them, and seek their own space. Some people need a period of withdrawal; in addition, it is important that the victim feel empowered to take some steps on their own to gain a sense of personal agency.
- Many treatments that are used quite routinely at later stages (e.g., exposure therapy; eye movement desensitization and reprocessing, EMDR; thought field therapy, TFT; and acupuncture) have not yet been demonstrated to be helpful, least of all when administered in the first hours and days after an event. Given that most survivors will recover without formal treatment, initiation of more intensive help should generally not be initiated during this acute care stage, unless there is evidence of problems warranting immediate intervention (e.g., suicidality, substance abuse problems, violence, exacerbation of chronic mental health problems, or impairment resulting in inability to care for self).
- The greatest risk to helpers may be "overhelping" or what some have called "the tyranny of urgency" – the tendency to go too far out of your way to help people do what they need to do for themselves, or even doing for them what can best be done by their own families and reference groups. Recovery ultimately may depend on fostering a sense of self-efficacy and mastery of the threat and challenge.
- Don't be too formal. Don't carry the badges of distance (such as a clipboard or a white coat) that might mark you as a removed clinical observer.

Don't push survivors to discuss or do something that they are reluctant to do

The greatest risk to helpers may be what some have called the "tyranny of urgency"

Tools
The following are services that can be provided during the acute support stage. Some activities may be applicable with every survivor while others may be used only in particular circumstances. It is up to the provider to identify which activities will be most useful.

Presence

Simply being present in a calm manner may be helpful to survivors. Some may not want to talk or listen, but may still benefit from the calming presence of another human being. In contrast, others may not be ready to talk and may not want you around. This is also acceptable. In this case, you may choose to take your leave, but leave these individuals with a handout that tells them how they can find additional assistance.

Answering Questions and Providing Basic Information

Before you initiate contact with survivors be sure you are educated in where to find information

There is an array of information that may be of use to survivors. Some may need basic information as to what is going on around them, what they need to do to ensure their safety or the safety of their loved ones, how to find out what has happened to their loved ones, what services are available to assist them, and/or where to go to find food, water, or clothing. Before initiating contact with survivors, be sure you are educated on such topics and are able to provide information and know where to find answers yourself.

Social Support

Practitioners can facilitate social support by encouraging the use of established support persons (family, loved ones, and friends) and available helping resources. It may also be useful to explore strategies for establishing new or interim social connections, and discussing ways to both give and receive social support. Many survivors will be actively using social supports, without the aid of a mental health expert. When this is not occurring, consider why and address the reasons as appropriate.

Brief Coping Advice

Many survivors may benefit from basic information on coping. Examples of positive coping include seeking social support, ensuring adequate rest and nutritious diet, and engaging in positive activities. These coping skills are fundamental, but they can be easily forgotten in the midst of disaster. Warnings against reliance on negative ways of coping may also be useful. Examples of negative coping include substance abuse, not caring for your basic needs, extreme avoidance behaviors, and engaging in risky activities. People may report that negative coping activities provide immediate relief, but may fail to realize they can cause more serious problems in the future.

Coping Skills Training

Provide psycho-educational handouts and teach coping skills in a manner that is applicable to the current circumstances

Some individuals may profit from short psycho-educational handouts regarding skills such as problem solving, anger management, and stress reduction and relaxation techniques. These skills can be taught in a manner that is applicable to current circumstances. For example, a practitioner could work with the survivor to employ problem solving techniques on an issue of particular salience to the survivor. Relaxation techniques can be tailored for the survivor's environment.

Summary

To summarize, the main focus of Stage 1 is on delivery of immediate practical services. The phrase *psychological first aid* (PFA) has come to refer to a set of such early services that are commonly provided in the immediate aftermath of disaster and terrorist attack. Recently, the term has been shaped to refer to a more specific set of principles as manualized by the National Child Traumatic Stress Network (NCTSN) and the National Center for Posttraumatic Stress Disorder (NCPTSD). This guide was released in September 2005 (shortly following the events of Hurricane Katrina) and served a wide variety of professionals responding to this disaster. The following list of 8 core actions of PFA, as described in the *Psychological First Aid: Field Operations Guide,* provides a succinct summary of many of the principles of the acute support discussed above:

There are 8 core actions that comprise PFA

1. *Contact and Engagement*
Goal: Respond to contacts initiated by affected persons, or initiate contacts in a nonintrusive, compassionate, and helpful manner.

2. *Safety and Comfort*
Goal: Enhance immediate and ongoing safety, and provide physical and emotional comfort.

3. *Stabilization (if necessary)*
Goal: To calm and orient emotionally overwhelmed/distraught survivors.

4. *Information Gathering: Current Needs and Concerns*
Goal: Identify immediate needs and concerns, gather additional information, and tailor PFA interventions.

5. *Practical Assistance*
Goal: To offer practical help to the survivor in addressing immediate needs and concerns.

6. *Connection with Social Supports*
Goal: To reduce distress by helping structure opportunities for brief or ongoing contacts with primary support persons or other sources of support, including family members, friends, and community helping resources.

7. *Information on Coping Support*
Goal: To provide the individual with information (including education about stress reactions and coping) that may help them deal with the event and its aftermath.

8. *Linkage with Collaborative Services*
Goal: To link survivors with needed services, and inform them about available services that may be needed in the future.

In addition to providing survivors with pragmatic and sensible assistance, the benefits of acute support are manifold. To start, acute support can be provided in a diverse range of settings ranging from the disaster scene to shelters to hospitals to homes. It can be used by itself or as part of a sequential treatment program. It is provided on an individual basis and does not require more than one session with the survivor. The philosophy of acute support (assisting with basic needs and coping ability) allows for the use of techniques in a flexible manner so that the practitioner can tailor the strategy for the individual. These techniques are not time consuming and allow the practitioner to make contact with many individuals over a relatively short period of time, thus increasing the number of individuals served. The techniques are reasonably simple and can be taught quickly and efficiently to new disaster mental health care workers. Additionally, information gathered from contacts with survivors can be used in triaging and making initial referrals or assessment for ongoing care.

4.1.2   Stage 2: Intermediate Support

Intermediate support is the second stage of the intervention program. The active ingredients of intervention at this stage are embodied in the therapeutic relationship. The Joint Task Force principles guiding intervention at this point all direct us to facilitating the relationship, overcoming ruptures to the relationship, and avoiding interpretations that might disrupt the relationship. At the point that a cooperative working relationship develops, the clinician can turn his/her attention to the task of helping the victim with the practical task of coping with daily stressors.

Cognitive and cognitive behavioral interventions have been shown across studies to out perform supportive counseling alone for those suffering from anxiety-based disorders such as ASD (Ehlers & Clark, 2003). Intermediate support can be provided following acute care within one-month post disaster by mental health professionals. Before intermediate care is provided, survivors should have their basic physical and safety needs met. While it is our hope that the employment of both relationship support and the specific skill training procedures of cognitive and cognitive-behavioral therapy will prevent the emergence of chronic symptoms, there is no viable scientific evidence to date that this is a realistic objective of this stage. What we can accomplish is facilitating a victim's hope through relationship support, while at the same time increasing coping skills and adaptability through specific cognitive-behavioral training.

Basic physical needs must be met before intermediate care is provided

Like the services provided in acute care, services associated with the intermediate stage of treatment can be used alone or as part of a sequential intervention program. If used as part of a sequential intervention program, intermediate care is suitable for survivors seen during the acute care stage and who meet any of the following five criteria:

Intermediate services can be used alone or as part of a sequential treatment program

1. A preevent history of personality disorder or treatment of severe psychiatric disorder;
2. Multiple symptoms of distress that impair current functioning and hamper reality testing
3. Failure to have available a stable source of social support from family or community agencies
4. A history of difficulties with people, with the law, and with authorities
5. A history of prior exposure to violence

As noted earlier, these criteria are directly based on the Joint Task Force report (Castonguay & Beutler, 2006a) review of prognostic indicators, supplemented by the long-term follow up of 9/11/2001 victims (Stuber et al., 2003; Galea, et al., 2003; Galea et al., 2002). Each of these five individual criteria is associated with an increase in the number of severe and persistent problems that survivors develop after a traumatic event.

The interventions and support provided at the intermediate stage (Stage 2) are based both on the prognostic principles of Stage 1 and the relationship factors that are associated with change in Stage 2. Intermediate support services can be provided in a variety of settings, but unlike acute care, requires repeat visits (from 3 to 5) with individual victims. The following are techniques that can be used to provide the level of intermediate support needed to assist survivors. Each technique should be used within the provision of intermediate support; however, the details associated with each technique can be determined by being sensitive to the needs of each individual. Many of these techniques and the patterns of their applications follow the suggestions of Bryant and colleagues (Bryant et al., 1999; Bryant et al., 2002; Bryant, Harvey et al., 1998). They have emerged directly as the result of controlled research demonstrating their efficacy for helping victims of trauma recover. While they have not been studied in terrorist-based trauma, there is reason to accept them as being empirically derived and supported.

> Many techniques have emerged directly as a result of controlled research demonstrating their efficacy for helping victims of trauma recover

Supportive and Collaborative Environment
Foster a supportive environment that provides the individual with an opportunity to feel as safe and comfortable as possible with you.

Communicating Basis for Treatment
Ask the individual what they are hoping to gain from their interaction with you. Incorporate this information into your decisions about what interventions you will be able to offer the individual and if you feel that those associated with intermediate support are applicable.

Psychoeducation
Provide the individual with psychoeducation on various topics (to be chosen based on the needs of the individual). Through this process, you will help them understand what they are experiencing. Topics could include any of the following (but this is by no means a complete list):
- Relationship between thoughts, emotions, and behaviors
- Thought intrusions
- Emotional numbing
- Avoidance
- Physical arousal
- Loss of interest
- Loss of appetite
- Constant worry
- Sleep difficulties
- Difficulty concentrating
- Depression
- Anger
- Positive and negative coping

Identifying and Assessing Thoughts

The practitioner can help the survivor identify the difference between thoughts and feelings and begin to label thoughts and feelings. After this is accomplished, the practitioner and survivor can discuss the validity of current thoughts.

Cognitive Restructuring

This portion of the intervention can be used to introduce survivors to their pattern of thoughts, emotions, and behaviors, and how changing thoughts may influence emotion and behavior. The practitioner can assist the individual in thinking rationally, using evidence to evaluate their thoughts and seeking alternative views.

Homework

Homework can be used (if practical) to assist the survivor in learning the techniques discussed in session.

Anxiety Management

The survivor can be taught techniques used to manage anxiety and stress. Examples of such techniques include exercises such as diaphragmatic breathing and progressive muscle relaxation. Information gathered through the intermediate support intervention can be used to assess the need for ongoing treatment (see Assessment).

Summary

There are a variety of tools that can be used at this stage. While the interventions suggested are based on research-informed principles, empirical support for their effectiveness in disaster contexts is not yet available. We have provided some suggestions for what interventions might be helpful, based largely on the demonstration of the efficacy of cognitive-behavioral approaches for more chronic posttrauma problems and on research on early intervention with ASD conducted by Bryant and colleagues, who have conducted randomized, controlled trials of the efficacy of these procedures with victims of various traumas (Bryant et al., 2002; Bryant et al., 1999, Bryant et al., 1998). Research conducted to date suggests that a CBT package can out perform supportive counseling alone for those suffering from ASD due to violent assault and accidents (Ehlers & Clark, 2003).

4.1.3   Stage 3: Ongoing Treatment

The specific and illustrative interventions that are recommended for application in the third stage of treatment have been shaped from the model of trauma treatment developed and researched by Bryant and colleagues. The adaptation of the interventions to comply with the differential treatment applications outlined by the Joint Task Force principles (Castonguay & Beutler, 2006a) are our own.

Bryant, Harvey, Dang, and Sackville (1998) compared the effectives of two treatments, CBT and supportive counseling (SC), for the treatment of ASD.

The CBT treatment included trauma education, relaxation training, imaginal exposure, cognitive restructuring, and in vivo exposure. The SC treatment included trauma education, problem solving skill instruction, and unconditional support. Unfortunately, no evidence was provided to ensure that therapeutic levels of relationship attachment and working alliance resulted from these procedures, and relationship factors remain confounded in the comparisons. Nonetheless, the results support the power and superiority of CBT-based treatments. While the authors acknowledge the limitations associated with the study, including small sample size and limited types of trauma events included, it remains a convincing argument for the use of CBT. In particular, this research represents some of the first applications of psychotherapy (outside of CISD) to the treatment of individuals during the early stage of intervention.

Moreover, follow up analyses clarified the components of the CBT treatment package. Bryant et al., (1999) reported that similar effects were obtained when the effects of prolonged exposure were compared with a combination of prolonged exposure and anxiety management, suggesting that exposure may be an important contributor to the beneficial effects of the treatment. Bryant et al., (2002) concluded that both exposure-based and cognitive restructuring interventions are effective components of the treatment package when addressing PTSD symptoms. We have relied on these demonstrations in suggesting that different clusters of procedures should be emphasized when tailoring treatment to victim characteristics such as coping style, as suggested by the Joint Task Force principles previously reviewed.

Stage 3 interventions are tailored to the needs of the client and are based heavily on CBT

In Stage 3, we tailor the intervention to the particular patient and his or her problems.

1. Anxiety Disorders

Among patients/victims with PTSD and no comorbid personality disorder, chemical abuse, or depression, a CBT package of interventions that combine exposure and coping interventions, such as that developed and used by Bryant and colleagues, is appropriate. The intensity, frequency, and duration of the intervention should be adapted to the patient's level of functional impairment.

2. Chemical Abuse/Dependency

Among patients/victims whose postadjustment period includes heavy use of illicit drugs or alcohol, adaptations should be made for both the level of impairment and for the level of resistance predicted to characterize their response and investment in treatment. The clinician should adapt the intensity of treatment, including the duration and frequency of sessions and the use combined treatments (e.g., group and individual therapy), for patients with severe impairments. Impairment can be roughly assessed by identifying the presence of few social supports, comorbidity, and chronic interpersonal problems. High levels of resistance to direction, particularly as indicated by a failure to do homework assignments, failure to keep appointments, anger at the therapist, and other signs of excessive interpersonal sensitivity, should serve as a cue for the clinician to take a nondirective and nonevocative stance in applying the procedures, and avoid direct guidance, excessive verbalizations, interpretations, or other interventions that emphasize therapist control and guidance.

3. Depression and Comorbidity

Among depressed patients, interventions should be modified as necessary to reflect patients' resistance levels, impaired functioning, and different coping styles. The intensity of treatment should be adapted to the level of impairment and the directiveness of the therapist's approach should be adapted to the level of the patients resistance to intervention and general interpersonal sensitivity. But, one should also take account of the need to adapt the focus of the intervention to the patient's tendency to rely on externalized or internalized strategies of coping. To accommodate this need, Stage 3 interventions are presented as contrasting lists of interventions to guide the treatment of those victims who tend to be externalized and impulsive, on the one hand, or internalized and self-reflective, on the other.

These lists of interventions for internalizing and externalizing victims/patients can be used separately to address particular patient's needs or they can be combined when patients seem receptive and in need of additional help.

4.1.4   Interventions for Internalizing Victims

The interventions for internalizing victims combine supportive procedures and prolonged exposure. Supportive interventions capitalize on relationship qualities and structure to promote change. Exposure procedures attempt to raise patients' awareness and tolerance for anxiety by reintroducing them to traumatic experiences. Thus, *the third stage of intervention is the first time that we recommend such reintroduction of feared experiences.* The general structure of sessions that emphasize this internal focus may be as follows, with more or less attention given to different components as time permits and as is consistent with the stage of intervention. Thus, early sessions would address more education and monitoring while later sessions would work more with exposure and coping training.

- Review medical/drug use status, homework, and motivation for change
- Education about important concepts in social support and symptom monitoring
- Provide a stable therapeutic environment by adherence to time limits and focus of the sessions on daily problems
- Address impediments to a stabilized external environment
- Provide practice in exposure using imaginal experiencing
- Provide support and reassurance
- Practice staying in the moment while anxiety passes
- Identify accomplishments and achievements to enhance self-esteem
- Plan next steps and make appointment for next session

Supportive Therapy

The components of supportive therapy include teaching the survivor to stay in the moment and wait for anxiety to pass or reduce. It may also include relaxation training and self-esteem building exercises. Also, the practitioner may instruct the survivor in the nature of self-talk and distraction, and may encourage him/her to seek support groups thereby enhancing their social support networks.

Providing support entails the use of a variety of procedures that are designed to help a person stay in the moment and feel encouraged. These include the use of reflection to identify and acknowledge the victim's feelings, and active listening and reframing until the victim believes that the clinician understands his or her concerns and fears. Victims can also be encouraged to seek out social support through recreation groups, self-help groups, or religious groups. Among chemical abusers, Alcoholics Anonymous or Narcotics Anonymous can provide such support. The mere presence of a supportive and caring person, in the body of the clinician, can help patients cope with the sequelae of trauma. Finally, contracting can help the victim work through problems, face fears, and stay in treatment as s/he adapts to the posttrauma demands of living.

Providing support entails a variety of procedures designed to help a person stay in the moment and feel encouraged

Training Victims to Stay in the Moment

Training victims to stay with their feelings and be in the moment is an educational process that comes with associated homework assignments. The nature of anxiety as an anticipatory response is explained. The clinician also explains that anxiety is incubated and increased whenever its presence is followed by avoidance, distraction, or withdrawal. The victim is instructed in how to monitor anxiety levels and to stop what they are doing when anxiety becomes noticeable. They are then trained to relax, breath, and stay in one place until they note a decrease of anxiety sensations. Practice in breathing smoothly, evenly, and consistently when under stress helps this process. Likewise, training in deep muscle relaxation provides an effective coping skill to use in times of stress, and the victim/patient can learn to stay focused on the anxiety itself while breathing and relaxing until the acute panic and need to withdraw or run away subsides.

Self-Esteem Training

Building self-esteem is a process that capitalizes on accomplishments and achievements. The victim is encouraged to start small, perhaps describing things that she does well or things that she aspires to learn to do well. Then the therapist helps the victim focus on small steps that will get her closer to her goal. It is helpful if the victim can find a support group to help with the process of taking these small steps while receiving encouragement and praise. Negative thoughts are targeted as causes of low self-esteem. They are identified through work with the clinician; after they are identified, a victim can be instructed in how to distract, replace, or reevaluate the thoughts. Finally, patients/victims are encouraged to use self-talk to guide themselves through a task, asking such questions as "What are my expectations?" "How realistic are they?" "What can I do to make a small change?" and "What is the next step to get through this?"

Building self-esteem capitalizes on accomplishments and achievements

Exposure

It is important that exposure is preceded by preparation. The clinician attempts to make several points before actual imaginal exposure is undertaken:
- Avoidance prevents you from understanding and processing the memory of the traumatic experience
- No matter how hard you try to push away thoughts about the trauma, they come back to you in distressing ways when you don't want them to

- These symptoms are a sign that the trauma is still "unfinished business"
- Therapy is a way to help you put your trauma into perspective, as well as reduce the amount of distress you feel when you are reminded of it
- I will be asking you to talk about your experience and memories of the traumatic event in detail
- We'll do this over and over until you feel more comfortable and less anxious about the trauma
- This approach has been found to be helpful and to result in memories becoming less upsetting; in turn, unpleasant thoughts, flashbacks, and nightmares become less frequent

The goal of therapy is to help victims unlearn the things that they very quickly learned during the traumatic experience

Victims/patients are reminded that the goal of therapy is to help them unlearn the things that they very quickly learned during traumatic experiences. It may be helpful to explain that one's body quickly learns to respond to perceived danger and to avoid these situations whenever possible. However, avoidance inevitably leads to more anxiety. The principles of extinction are explained, with examples, and then the process of imaginal exposure is described.

Imaginal exposure is initiated and is done several times per session until anxiety reduces. This procedure entails recalling a traumatic event and holding it in one's mind for as long as it takes to notice a reduction in one's emotional level. The patient may use a single event repeatedly or embellish it by including similar instances in which fear has been present.

The victim is reminded as often as necessary that exposure is a means of teaching the body that one can think about fearful things without being harmed. Confronting anxiety reduces the patient's sense of danger and teaches him or her that things are not as dangerous as they may seem. The patients/victims may be told that by trying to confront these situations in their memory, they will learn that nothing bad will happen to them when they confront their fears. They are also cautioned that they will be asked to remember things that remind them of the trauma, or deliberately remember the trauma while staying in the moment until their anxiety passes.

Victims are asked to expose themselves to unpleasant thoughts and memories, note any thought intrusions, and retrain themselves to focus on the anxiety events in a controlled manner until such memories are no longer distressing. They are also told that there may have been subtle changes in the ways in which they see the world, making it important to examine thoughts and beliefs, and then challenge and change those that are not realistic or helpful. The clinician helps the victim/patient identify these beliefs and evaluate how realistic and unrealistic their assumptions are. Thus, the therapist may ask such questions as: "What do you think would happen if you have this thought?" "How realistic is that?" "Is there any other way to view this?" "What is the worst thing that could happen?" "How likely is that to occur?"

4.1.5   Interventions for Externalizing Victims

The treatment of externalizing victims follows a similar outline to the foregoing one, but with emphasis on learning new skills and controlling impulsive behavior. The structure of the sessions include the following components:

- Reviewing medical records and activities
- Presenting the description and rationale of treatment using the A-B-C model (antecedents, beliefs, and consequences)
- Introducing or checking the patient's daily activity schedule
- Reviewing thought records
- Evaluating past homework assignments, e.g., tracking behaviors and associated thoughts
- Providing supportive therapy

The initial review of medical status and activities is similar to that used in the treatment of internalizing patients. From this review, an agenda of topics can be defined and each problem can be prioritized. This should be checked each time the clinician meets with the victim/patient in order to monitor progress.

It also will be noted that supportive therapy is used with both internalizing and externalizing patients. Indeed, in both cases, the amount of supportive therapy provided will be a direct function of resistance and the interpersonal hypersensitivity of the victim/patient.

Rationale for Treatment
Patients benefit from understanding the rationale behind the treatment. For these interventions, the emphasis is placed on the A-B-C model of cognitive therapy. The relationship between events and thoughts and between thoughts and feelings/behaviors is explained. It is emphasized that feelings and behaviors that cause one trouble are never the direct result of events, but instead are the products of what we believe about the situations and the events that occur. Patients/victims are asked if they understand this way of viewing their difficulties, and any concerns or questions they have are addressed and answered. It is important that this model is adequately explained and is sufficiently well accepted that one can begin the process of treatment.

The emphasis of interventions for externalizing victims is on learning new skills and controlling impulsive behavior

Daily Activity Schedule
To help patients learn the relationship between thoughts and behaviors, they are taught to record, using a daily activity schedule, various events that occur during the time between appointments and how they felt about these events. Daily activity schedules can both identify progress toward particular behavioral goals and identify those behaviors and activities that impede effective functioning. Social activities are particularly important to track among victims who are depressed after a traumatic event. Engagement in social activities and success in interpersonal relationships are readily observed as the daily records are discussed.

Thought Records
A daily record of anxious or depressive thoughts are also kept with an associated recording of the feelings and actions that accompanied these thoughts. The clinician works with the patient to identify unrealistic or dysfunctional thoughts as well as recurrent patterns of thought that interfere with progress in therapy. When dysfunctional and distorted thoughts are identified, the clinician helps the victim evaluate their validity by asking questions such as:

- Is this thought true or always true?
- Would everyone agree with your belief?
- Is there any other way to see it?
- What is the evidence – for and against – this belief or thought?

When reviewing these records, the clinician notes how events are interpreted, with special reference to any systematic and recurrent ways of personalizing or disowning blame and responsibility. As time goes on, these records are expanded to include suggestions for new thoughts to practice when bad things happen.

Homework

At the conclusion of each session, the patient and clinician work together to develop a homework assignment for the victim. These assignments aim to develop the skills necessary to address deficits and difficulties in interpersonal relationships, and they also help the client identify and practice new ways of perceiving and evaluating negative experiences.

Insight and exploratory interventions for internalizers, and skill building and control exercises for externalizers, can be concluded with a discussion of what the survivor has learned and the attributions s/he uses to understand any change that has occurred. Additionally, the practitioner and survivor can discuss ways in which the survivor can continue their work once sessions have concluded and what the survivor can do should if s/he starts feeling like s/he did prior to her/his work with the practitioner.

Intervention continues until substantial change is noted or until a transfer to a different intervention

The third stage of intervention continues until substantial change is achieved in the dominant symptoms or until a transfer to a different form of intervention is indicated by circumstances. In many trauma situations, the clinicians providing these services are volunteers who must leave the site of the event before the victim has completed therapy. In these cases, a transfer to a different therapist with similar goals and objectives is desirable.

4.2   Mechanisms of Action

The principle-driven techniques described above include a range of mechanisms of action through which change occurs. As noted earlier, it is common for survivors of mass violence and other trauma to experience acute stress reactions. The processes by which these reactions are reduced for most – and maintained or exacerbated for some – are not well understood, but models of posttrauma responding have included classical conditioning, posttrauma appraisal, coping processes, self-efficacy, loss or preservation of resources, and faulty processing of trauma-related emotions. Based on existing models, several mechanisms of action may be hypothesized to determine the impact of helping procedures (note that many helping activities simultaneously address multiple mechanisms of action):

Many helping activities simultaneously address multiple mechanisms of action

4.2.1   Reduction of Physiological Arousal

The experience of continuing hyperarousal following trauma may maintain a client's belief that the world is dangerous, provide a stimulus for negative self-labels, interfere with emotional processing of the traumatic memories, provide additional fear conditioning trials, increase the client's sense of helplessness, reduce self-efficacy, and motivate maladaptive avoidance coping behaviors. Successful reduction of physiological anxiety and arousal may reduce the likelihood and/or intensity of these effects. Such reduction may occur through direct methods, such as relaxation or breathing training, cognitive therapy, or medications. It may also result more indirectly from simply working with a sympathetic and caring therapist.

> The experience of hyperarousal following trauma may maintain a client's belief that the world is a dangerous place

Some of the processes of acute support and PFA, such as increasing sense of safety, connecting with social supports, giving accurate information, and identifying helping coping actions, may all serve to reduce arousal.

4.2.2   Reduction of Fear of Acute Stress Reactions

Negative interpretations of stress reactions (e.g., "I'm going crazy" or "I'm weak") reinforce and maintain a client's ongoing sense of threat. They may increase a client's sense of danger and unpredictability, and undermine her/his capacity to cope. They may also serve as a motivation to avoid contact with others, discussion of the events themselves, and any emotional engagement that is associated with memories of the traumatic event. Interventions address these negative self-statements by assessing, educating about, and normalizing stress reactions. They strengthen clients' perceived ability to manage their reactions by teaching adaptive self-talk and anxiety management methods. When survivors are linked for social support with others who are being similarly affected, the sharing of experiences can significant reduce fear of these physiological reactions and the problematic appraisals associated with them. Exposure interventions show survivors that they can indeed experience feelings and memories without going crazy, and that they are strong enough to cope with the arousal they experience.

> Interventions address negative self-statements by assessing, educating about, and normalizing stress reactions

4.2.3   Change in Negative Trauma-Related Appraisals

Beyond appraisals of stress reactions, there are many negative trauma-related cognitions that can create a sense of continuing threat and help maintain stress reactions. These can be related to guilt- or anger-related beliefs, negative views of oneself or one's behaviors, negative beliefs about other people, or excessively negative views of a changed future resulting from the trauma. Often these appraisals go beyond the available evidence, ignore aspects of the traumatic experience itself, are excessively extreme or generalized (e.g., "I'm weak, a coward, and bad person"), or make unwarranted assumptions about the future. Many of the interventions described in this book address appraisals in direct and indirect ways. Cognitive interventions directly focus on education about the role of appraisals in recovery, identification of problematic beliefs and judgments, and development of repertoires for challenging these beliefs. More broadly, much trauma-related education provides the survivor with adaptive ways of understanding his or her experience. Social support transactions often help the survivor to review negative appraisals, as do successful coping efforts and resumption of rewarding activities. Anxiety reduction techniques can often help clients cope with anxious thinking.

4.2.4   Increase in Perceived Self-Efficacy

Self-efficacy is a central determinant of posttrauma functioning

One particularly important class of appraisals is that related to self-efficacy for coping with a traumatic event and its effects. As noted earlier, Foa and colleagues have hypothesized that a belief that "one's self is totally incompetent" is a primary dysfunctional cognition that may mediate development of PTSD, and social cognitive theory stresses perception of self-efficacy as a central determinant of posttrauma functioning (Benight & Bandura, 2004).

Many interventions can affect self-efficacy. Skills training related to self-talk or physical relaxation provides clients with tools to manage their reactions to memories of traumatic events; if these tools are perceived as successful, they will often have a direct impact on self-efficacy judgments. Coping advice can have the same effect. Social support interventions can enhance efficacy by providing survivors with knowledge about how others are coping. If counseling efforts result in symptom improvement, efficacy ratings are likely to increase.

4.2.5   Increase in Positive, Rewarding Activities

The depression associated with exposure to trauma (as well as the disruption of community structures themselves in mass disaster) can result in reduced participation in activities that could help improve mood, increase sense of personal competence, and restore sense of meaning and purpose. To the extent that discussions of coping involve encouragement, as appropriate, to return to meaningful activities, depression may be ameliorated. If participation in these activities (including mutual aid activities related to rebuilding an affected community) provides positive experiences for survivors, this can provide evidence that can challenge some negative appraisals (e.g., "my life is ruined forever"), bolster positive self-efficacy, improve depressed mood, kindle social reengagement and support, and provide more opportunities for emotion processing through discussion with others.

4.2.6   Reduction in Maladaptive Avoidance

Some patterns of posttrauma coping may be associated with development of chronic problems. These would include ongoing use of alcohol and drugs to cope, continuing withdrawal from social and other potentially rewarding activities, and extreme emotional avoidance. Self-medication of stress reactions may result in impairment of coping efforts, additional negative consequences (e.g., social, occupational, financial, legal), and exacerbation or development of substance abuse problems. Social withdrawal may result in loss of social support, loss of instrumental help from others (resource loss), and loss of access to rewarding social activities. Extreme avoidance of trauma-related emotions and memories may prevent engagement with the traumatic memory and thus interfere with emotion processing. The interventions discussed in this book may help reduce problematic coping after a traumatic event by providing brief advice about positive and negative coping actions, routinely assessing use of substances/previous substance abuse problems, encouraging social contact and support, pointing out emotional avoidance and addressing this problem if indicated, teaching positive coping actions that can replace negative ones, intervening to establish or facilitate social contact and support, and prompting emotion processing by continuing to discuss the impact of the event. Exposure interventions explicitly reduce emotional avoidance by helping the survivor experience trauma-related emotions and process the traumatic memory.

Exposure interventions explicitly reduce emotional avoidance

4.2.7   Emotional Processing of Traumatic Memories

For some survivors, part of the process of recovery from trauma may involve the emotional processing of a memory characterized by intense emotion, the sense of reliving the trauma, and flashbacks. This process can result from direct discussion of traumatic experiences with a helper (as in exposure interventions), or from less formal discussions with support persons in the natural environment; it may also occur when various helping actions lead the survivor to dwell upon his or her experiences. Emotion processing involves direct emotional engagement with the memory that may help organize the memory, integrate it with other memories, and derive a set of recovery-supporting appraisals (e.g., a balanced view about the dangerousness of the world and competency of the self). This process can result in an extinction of conditioned emotional responses, as the individual revisits the traumatic experience and learns that stimuli associated with it are not dangerous.

4.2.8   Reduction of Negative Consequences of Traumatic Events/Ongoing Adversity

For many trauma survivors, life after trauma may present many difficulties and continuing adversities. These adversities can include ongoing medical treatment, financial problems, challenges of adaptation to new environments, interpersonal relationship problems, and continuing posttraumatic stress symptoms. Continuing posttrauma problems contribute to a sense of continuing threat and constitute ongoing stressors. Therefore, interventions posttrauma must focus on reducing these ongoing negative consequences and continuing loss of resources as much as possible. In fact, during PFA, the primary focus is on addressing the pragmatic needs of survivors, through problem-solving and linkage with services, social supports, counseling opportunities, and other activities designed to restore some lost resources.

Posttrauma interventions must continue to focus on reducing negative consequences and loss of resources

4.2.9   The Role of Principles of Change

On a more global level, and from the standpoint of the operation of principles of change, there are at least three explanations for how the treatment program identified here works. One of these explanations emphasizes the role of therapeutic relationships. Indeed, there is reasonable evidence that relationship factors are important in promoting change (e.g., Norcross, 2002). The current program capitalizes on the nature of relationships that have been found to be healing.

A second explanation attributes change to the motivation and involvement of the patient and therapist. There is no doubt that these contributors are involved (Norcross, 2002). The current program incorporates principles based on participant qualities to direct the therapist to identify these characteristics and employ them in ways that promote change.

The third explanation is that the specific techniques of PFA, skill training, support, and exposure, are effective in facilitating change and improvement. While most treatments do not differ from one another in efficacy, it is unlikely that all procedures are equally effective, and a strong body of research has accumulated supporting the value of the techniques that we have described here (Chambless & Ollendick, 2001; Nathan & Gorman, 2002).

4.3   Efficacy and Prognosis

Most people improve following mass trauma by relying on social networks, families, and support systems. Only about +20% have lingering problems, an increase of about 5–10% over incidence rates before the mass trauma. Thus, treatment is targeted for these +20% with the hope of reducing the likelihood and severity of their suffering.

Resilience is high after a disaster and the efficacy of a number of treatments requires additional investigation

The best available evidence for the efficacy of the interventions obtained here, drawn from many different sources, is around 80%. Meta-analyses (e.g., Smith, Glass, & Miller, 1980; Wampold, 2001) as well as comprehensive reviews of specific literature (Beutler, Clarkin, & Bongar, 2000) find that this estimate characterizes treatments for most types of depression and anxiety. However, recurrence rates may be slightly higher among chemically dependent patients and recovery rates slightly lower, than for those with anxiety and depression. Abstinence rates following treatment for chemical dependency are in the 30% range.

However, none of these estimates fully address treatments that encompass the range of variables that are embodied in the Joint Task Force principles. Some suggestive and preliminary evidence of the additive and collective effect of adding patient, treatment, relationship, and therapy fit variables across treatment, suggests that the overall efficiency of the treatments are improved, with the collection of variables accounting for from 35% to over 90% of the variance in short- and long-term outcomes (Beutler, Moleiro et al., 2003).

At the level of assessing the procedures and techniques that we have outlined, the immediate stage interventions outlined above have, to date, not been subjected to empirical evaluation. The manualization of PFA can be expected to prompt evaluation of the approach, and it is important that the impact of key elements of these immediate services, such as brief coping advice, be examined in research.

Stage 2 interventions have been studied on a limited basis, primarily in nondisaster contexts. Studies cited above by Bryant and colleagues have suggested the utility of cognitive-behavioral interventions combining education, exposure, cognitive therapy, and anxiety management, and other researchers have obtained results with other trauma populations that suggest that similar interventions may help prevent PTSD (e.g., Bisson, Shepherd, Joy, Probert, & Newcombe, 2004; Foa, Hearst-Ikeda, & Perry, 1995). Nonetheless, these findings require replication in other settings, exploration of the factors that affect their impact, and extension to the real-world contexts of terrorism and disaster.

Stage 3 interventions have received the most validation. A number of practice guidelines now refer to evidence-based treatments for PTSD (e.g., Foa, Keane, & Friedman, 2000; VA-DoD Clinical Practice Guideline Working Group, 2003), with exposure therapy, cognitive therapy, stress inoculation training, eye movement desensitization reprocessing, and specific medication treatments often identified as efficacious. Again, most studies to date have not focused on survivors of terrorist events or large-scale disasters. Some evidence that cognitive-behavioral treatment for terrorism-related PTSD can reduce symptoms was provided by Gillespie, Duffy, Hackmann, and Clark (2002). They studied survivors of a 1998 terrorist bombing in Omagh, Northern Ireland, who received cognitive-behavioral therapy between 1 and 34 months (median 10 months) postattack. Ninety-one patients who met the criteria for PTSD resulting from the bombing received 2–78 sessions (with a mean of 8) of a treatment which combined imaginal exposure with cognitive therapy. Seventy-eight patients demonstrated significant pre-post improvement on standardized measures of symptoms, with an effect size for improvement in PTSD symptoms of 2.47, comparable to or larger than controlled trials of cognitive-behavioral therapy for PTSD.

Stage 3 interventions have received the most research validation

4.4   Variations and Combinations of Methods

To be maximally effective, the three stages of care described above must be integrated into a comprehensive program of care for survivors. They are intended to form a system of stepped care in which (1) all survivors receive brief acute support help, (2) individuals judged at risk or desirous of counseling are monitored and/or receive intermediate Stage 2 care, and (3) persons still experiencing difficulty at later times despite receipt of services at the two earlier stages (or having failed to seek previous care) are offered Stage 3 interventions. To date, however, real integration has seldom been achieved. In part this is because individuals and agencies providing acute support services (e.g., outreach workers, mental health responders working in shelters) are not the same group of providers/agencies who provide acute care, and postacute care services may be delivered by yet a third group of providers. Moreover, most responders and providers are relatively unfamiliar with some of the Stage 2 and Stage 3 services described here. Acute support services as commonly delivered are similar to those advocated here, although manualization of PFA is a recent development. The identification and monitoring (as opposed to

To be maximally effective, the 3 stages of care must be integrated into a comprehensive program of care for survivors

treatment) of individuals who may be at risk for continuing problems has not be widely implemented, partly because of logistical problems in following up with survivors in mass casualty situations. Research on Stage 2 services employing anxiety management and brief cognitive therapy methods have only recently been initiated, so these approaches have not been widely disseminated. Application of components of the Stage 2 and 3 interventions in which well-studied interventions are brought to bear on survivors whose problems are continuing for several months posttrauma was seen in New York following the World Trade Center terrorist attacks, when community practitioners were trained in delivery of evidence-based treatments for PTSD.

Disaster mental health response in the U.S. is beginning to approximate this integration: PFA-compatible care is widely offered, and crisis counseling services offered in federally declared disasters are increasingly likely to use Stages 1 and 2 helping procedures and principles. And, as noted above, communities affected by mass disaster are beginning to implement programs to train local practitioners in Stages 2 and 3 interventions. These developments are being accelerated by research with trauma survivors in other settings in which integrated systems of care are being tried (e.g., with injury survivors in hospital settings, cf. Zatzick et al., 2004).

4.5   Problems in Carrying out the Treatments

Providers face key challenges in carrying out the interventions outlined above.

4.5.1   Motivation to Use Services

Challenges include motivation to use services, drop out rates, logistics and availability of trained providers

A central barrier to provision of many of the services outlined above is the fact that many individuals affected by trauma will not accept or use available mental health services. Sometimes this is related to a lack of understanding of personal stress reactions and/or lack of awareness of existing services. Even when aware, many survivors are reluctant to seek mental health services because of a lack of knowledge about what takes place in counseling, a reluctance to label themselves as having a mental health problem, or perceived social stigma associated with using such services. This obstacle to delivery of care has resulted in routine implementation of programs that actively reach out to survivors rather than wait passively for individuals to seek help. Outreach workers knock on doors, liaise with local organizations, and go to places where survivors gather. Services are marketed via local media. Attempts are made at all levels to destigmatize services, normalize help-seeking, and avoid mental health language and trappings.

4.5.2   Drop Out Rates

In their review of early psychological intervention, McNally et al. (2003) suggest that the problem of high drop out rates associated with CBT is an unresolved issue that needs further examination. These authors report drop out rates being higher in Bryant et al. (1999) and Foa et al. (2002) than in studies relying less on exposure and posit that cognitive therapy may be less stressful and thus have lower drop out rates.

4.5.3   Logistics of Mass Casualty Events

The scale of mass disasters creates challenges for delivering the kinds of services advocated here. The supply of mental health responders is often inadequate to meet the demand for services after a major disaster. In some events, obstacles to travel, or perceptions of ongoing environmental danger (e.g., continuing risk from terrorist attack or toxic exposure) may interfere with access to survivors. Both telephone (e.g., Somer et al., 2005) and internet interventions are likely to see increasing application in such circumstances. Future research should focus on testing these modalities following a terror event.

4.5.4   Availability of Trained Service Providers

Most mental health providers have not been trained in evidence-based treatments or in the evidence-informed services outlined above. But some recent evidence suggests that mental health professionals can be rapidly trained to deliver these treatments. For example, Gillespie, Duffy, Hackmann, and Clark (2002) evaluated cognitive therapy as a intervention with survivors of the 1998 Omagh terrorist bombing in Northern Ireland who met criteria for PTSD. Therapists were National Health Service mental health providers with no previous experience treating trauma. These therapists were trained rapidly via workshops and a mix of ongoing face-to-face and telephone supervision. Results indicated that these practitioners were effective in significantly reducing PTSD symptoms among bombing survivors.

Most mental health providers are not trained in evidence-based treatments

4.6.   Additional Tools for Responders

Disaster mental health responders may function in a variety of roles in addition to that mental health provider. Psychology, as a field, is varied and offers a great number of exciting and interesting roles for the interested individual; likewise, disaster mental health offers many different ways in which psychologists and other mental health providers can be helpful. For example, a mental health volunteer may chose to provide his/her service via interactions with survivors, but may also serve in advisory roles at the command-level, operate at a team management level, consult with a city manager regarding the ongoing mental health concerns of a surrounding community, and so forth. The role of mental health specialists in disaster response can potentially be as varied as individual interests allow. Thus, having tools with which to provide care to survivors is important, but is not the only set of useful information from which a mental health responder can benefit.

4.6.1   Learning from Experience

Providers responding to Hurricane Katrina were eager to share their experiences with the authors and others in hope that it could help other responders and assist in future response efforts. The feedback received from such individuals is listed below in an effort to encourage discussion and collaboration, but do not necessarily reflect the views of the authors or publisher.

Most large response organizations neglect to offer training in mental health interventions other than CISD

First, providers note that large response organizations neglect to offer training or services in mental health interventions other than CISD, and many of these groups remain committed to potentially outdated approaches. Though providers may want such training and experience, they are often torn as to whether or not their energy and resources should be directed towards learning about programs they would not be permitted to use during a disaster response.

Secondly, many responders who have been trained in trauma response were frustrated by being turned away by large organizations. Would-be volunteers who report having tried repeatedly to be of service were told they would be contacted soon but were never again contacted.

Third, field providers have noted that evacuees/survivors reportedly have little interest in "going to talk with someone," and few specifically sought mental health assistance. A large portion of mental health volunteers' energies appeared to be directed towards pharmacological and substance dependence problems. Evacuees not facing such difficulties were reportedly more open to "wandering" professionals (professionals who walked around the shelters and made direct contact with evacuees) employing an approach similar to the traditional fundamentals of acute care/PFA, rather than having to approach walled off areas in pursuit of mental health services.

Additionally, it appears that the assistance projects run by smaller organizations seemed to have left responders with more favorable impressions regarding the degree of services provided to evacuees. Frustration with the media's portrayal of the plight of evacuees, often inaccurate and sensationalized, were commonly shared by nonmental health volunteers as well.

Early and effective community response is one of the most valuable aspects of emergency response

From such anecdotal reports, it appears that early and effective community response is one of the most valuable aspects of emergency response. For example, after Hurricane Katrina, the entire Houston community seemed to have stepped forward to assist the evacuees. Residents opened their homes to both evacuees and volunteers, and the general atmosphere of the community, as reported by numerous volunteers, was characterized by warm welcomes, can-do attitudes, and genuine concern for the well-being of others.

Some responder's advocate for organizational philosophies that are pragmatic, open, nonterritorial, and which encourage an inclusive team approach to tasks and activities. A key factor in the success of some programs appears to be respect – for coworkers, other professionals, and for those who receive services, as well as for the ever growing efforts to improve technology within the disaster mental health field.

The following is a list of general guidelines derived from the real-world experience of emergency responders, including Palo Alto Medical Reserve Corps (PAMRC) staff, as well as from the *Psychological First Aid: Field Operations Guide* (NCTSN & NCPTSD, 2005). This list may be useful for practitioners in shaping their approach to emergency mental health care. These principles have been affectionately labeled "Field Smarts," and they are the core skills needed for emergency mental health response.

4.6.2   Field Smarts

- Always consider your safety as well as the safety of the survivor. If you identify a threat to anyone's safety, make sure the appropriate individuals are notified so that actions can be taken to address the threat.
- If you encounter someone who is hurt, seek immediate medical care. Consider employing basic first aid principles such as CPR, remaining with the survivor (if the scene is safe), and sending someone for help. You can receive training in first aid through various organizations including the American Red Cross, and it may be wise to do so should you be interested in responding to disasters.
- Model behavior and reactions that are calm, respectful, patient, receptive, and compassionate while still maintaining the ability to be assertive, act quickly, and manage your time.
- Be prepared for uncertainty in all aspects of the situation at hand.
- Operate within the structure of your overseeing response organization and address high risk behavior by employing your organization's risk management strategy.
- Take time to observe a situation before you make yourself a part of it. Watching how individuals interact or avoid one another can help you choose your own next steps.
- Recognize that people will deal with trauma in individual ways, and that you may need to correspondingly take different approaches with different people.

  "Field Smarts" are core skills needed by emergency disaster mental health responders

- Establish positive rapport quickly. Begin by introducing yourself and the organization you work for. Consider the stereotypes of mental health when describing your purpose. It may be best to simply say you are checking to see how people are doing and are available to help.
- Survivors may have just experienced losing much sense of control over their lives. Bombarding them with directions, orders, or "you should's" may not be well received. Instead, ask permission to talk with them. If it seems they would benefit from additional information (e.g., information about positive coping), ask if they would like to learn about how some other people have coped with trauma. Offer your assistance, but understand and accept that it is up to the individual to choose whether or not he or she wants to receive assistance.
- The use of psychological jargon should be avoided. Instead, use vocabulary that can be easily understood by a nonmental health professional.
- Similarly, don't pathologize reactions and avoid the use of labels such as "symptom" and "disorder."
- If you are providing information, have handouts available. People may quickly forget what you have said regardless of the clarity of your communication. Handouts provide an opportunity for them to refresh their memory, even months or years after your meeting.

- Remain cognizant and respectful of cultural differences that may affect various reactions following a traumatic event. Take steps to learn about the cultural groups that you will be helping.
- Be knowledgeable about the population you are targeting. Understand that there are significant differences in approaches/activities with adults versus children, first responders versus the general population, and so forth.
- Informally gather information that can assist in assessment and referral efforts.
- Operate within your professional context and expertise, and avoid making assumptions or statements of fact about someone's reactions or what s/he is experiencing.
- If you want to begin working in a disaster mental health role (or work with a population with which you are unfamiliar), seek education and mentorship.
- Act ethically, abide by your professional guidelines, and be aware of legal and liability issues.
- Don't be afraid to admit to not knowing an answer, but do try to seek the answer should such an effort be warranted.
- Be prepared to make referrals and educate yourself with key information (where the first aid station is, how to get help if needed, etc.).
- Closely attend to and monitor your own reactions and seek assistance if needed. Take your own advice. Don't let yourself get in the way of being helpful to others or yourself; employ self-care and positive coping.

4.6.3   Self-Care

It is no great secret that those in the disaster response field work in harsh environments that challenge the strength of even the hardiest and most experienced of responders. What follows is a summary of information on preparing for disasters, including facts about coping and self-care that can be useful for responders.

To take care of others you must first take care of yourself

The emergency response organization one chooses to volunteer with may have guidelines in place to assist in preparing for volunteer services. Preparation falls into 3 categories: notification of intention, gathering materials, and ongoing education and training.

Once an individual has decided to volunteer as a mental health responder, regardless of the volunteer role chosen, it is important to discuss such a desire with one's family and employer. For example, is there someone available to assist the family while the volunteer is away? Is there someone who is willing to oversee the volunteer's clients while they are away? In this way, one can make a disaster preparation plan specific to the occasion of deployment. This will not only help the volunteer focus on her/his upcoming response effort, but will also help significant others in their life prepare for the volunteer's absence. This is also a good time to ensure that the family has a plan should disaster strike close to home.

To save time, it may be useful to prepare response materials prior to receiving a call for deployment. What might go in such a packet? Certainly anything deemed necessary by the overseeing response organization: This may include documentation of your credentials, general handouts, a notebook and writing utensils, your organization's guidelines for care, key contacts, and this book or other professional materials you may find helpful when in the field. Additionally, one might also include items such as a packet of Kleenex, a calling card, a bottle of water, a snack, business cards, important personal phone numbers, a cell-phone charger, and so forth. If working at the command level, you will need information on media communication, talking points, or other materials that address your specialty. Ideally, the "disaster bag" can serve as a disaster response survival bag. Bring what it is needed, but try to bring only those items that you are genuinely likely to use.

Participating in ongoing education and training is essential to preparation. Attend courses and seminars hosted by the main response organization and others as well. Find a mentor who can provide supervision, helpful hints, and feedback. Make use of opportunities to attend events like disaster simulations or drills. The more someone knows and the more they practice, the more potential there is for an individual to feel confident when he or she arrives on scene. Learning can be facilitated through participation, but also through teaching; some providers may want to consider volunteering to instruct others about effective ways to help individuals who have been traumatized by disasters or terror. Some may also chose to get involved at higher levels in their organizations by volunteering to take on management roles and effect valuable changes. Ultimately, however, the goal is to do whatever it takes to stay current on the latest techniques and developments in the trauma recovery field.

Participation in ongoing education and training is essential to the preparation of a responder

Coping and self-care begins during preparation; by preparing as best one can, the individual is taking steps to reduce potential stress. Taking proactive steps to combat stress is a fundamental coping skill for disaster responders.

Try to work with a partner whenever possible. Though often you will not be able to see survivors together, having someone with whom to share experiences and collaborate will ease the burden of being a caregiver. In addition, partners can also watch out for one another and help each other remember to attend to self-care and monitor personal stress reactions.

Many people already know what types of stress-management techniques work best for them, but don't forget to use these techniques when responding to a disaster. Taking frequent breaks, eating well and regularly, and getting enough sleep are essential to maintaining well-being and strength. Practicing stress management techniques will help ensure that these basic self-care activities are not forgotten.

Though the lists of self-care and coping tools are long, some are more applicable to disaster response situations than others. For example, it is unlikely that there be a lot of spare time to engage in a pleasant activity such as visiting a museum, but it is likely (if made a priority) that there will be time for a less resource-consuming activity such as calling home to talk with family, listening to a favorite CD, or reading a book. Other handy activities that contribute to positive coping and self-care include journaling, self-reflection, talking to coworkers, exercise, participating in a group activity, relaxation exercises, laughing, prayer, and meditation.

Watch for negative coping reactions in yourself as well as victims. Be aware of any increase in substance use. Also, watch for isolation and withdrawal, self-destructive and high risk behaviors, and the tendency to work around the clock. Partners can help one another monitor for such things.

Coping and self-care aren't just important while during disaster response, but afterwards as well. Many people experience a variety of reactions when they return home, and it may take some time to adjust to being home again. For example, some disaster responders report feeling a bit depressed or questioning their world view and values. Even if away just a short while, the intensity of the disaster relief experience may contribute significantly to postdisaster response reactions. Continue to be mindful of your reactions and take whatever steps are necessary to positively cope with the feelings that emerge upon your return. When appropriate, when returning home if not before, it may be helpful to discuss the efficacy of the preparation plan with both family and employers and to make changes accordingly. Additionally, it may not hurt to express gratitude to those who supported your response efforts (family, friends, coworkers etc.). After all, it is often those behind the scenes that make it possible for responders to assist victims in times of need. Finally, mental health responders should remember to seek assistance if concerned about their own reactions.

Many people experience reactions when they return home and it may take some time to adjust to being home again

Case Vignettes

The following case vignettes are intended as thought experiments to help readers imagine how they might use this program following a mass trauma. We understand that there are many variables that influence how the provider program can be applied, so these vignettes are by no means concrete examples of what *should* be done. However, they serve as examples of what *could* be done by psychologists and other mental health professionals using this program.

Vignette 1: Mary

Mary is a 60 year old Hispanic female who survived the Oklahoma terrorist attack. At the point we meet her, she has been brought to a shelter within hours after the attack. Assume that you've been on-scene at the shelter for about 1 hour and have so far been able to help survivors find fresh water, first aid, services to assist them in locating missing family members, fresh water, and to address other critical needs. You have access to a variety of handouts, including one that lists community resources. Assume that your response organization has procedures in place for collecting contact information from those survivors with whom you come into contact, and has recently put into place a process by which follow-up contacts can be made regarding mental health needs. When you check-in, the shelter coordinator has suggested that you make contact with Mary. Also, assume that you have been asked to see Mary because the shelter coordinator is concerned about Mary's vacant expression, muted affect, and difficulty in responding to questions. For some reason, Mary has stood out in the coordinator's mind despite the coordinator's consuming and fast-paced responsibilities in setting up and running the shelter.

The scene is chaotic at the shelter,. You hear crying and angry outbursts from survivors, and at least half of the people you see somehow look a bit lost, even the volunteers. Others are sharply focused on the task at hand. You see people from all walks of life in varying degrees of distress and disarray. As you walk thought the shelter, you make a mental note of those individuals potentially exhibiting acute stress reactions that you will want to contact, and you remain vigilant for those individuals who may require immediate care. You find Mary by herself, leaning with her back against a wall.

Comment

In applying the intervention program proposed in this volume, your first task is to introduce yourself, open the door for a conversation with Mary, and thereafter to gather information that will help determine if she needs immediate treatment or simply needs to be followed as the situation unfolds. The third objective is to put Mary in contact with those resources that will be necessary to address her physical an safety needs.

Because of her muteness, the concern with severity of the problem and the immediacy of needed care is paramount. We recommend you approach her with a calm, nonthreatening voice and try to establish rapport quickly. If she does not respond favorably to your introduction and does not want to speak with you at that time, you might choose to let her know that you will check-in with her again later and leave to work with other survivors. If Mary responds positively to your introduction, you will want to take the opportunity to engage her in a brief discussion. Avoid talking about the event, but begin asking her how she is doing and, as soon as you have an opening, ask about what seems to be bothering her most at this time. Discretion and clinical judgment are necessary, even at this early stage in your contact, and it is not wise to assume that her odd behavior is necessarily related to the traumatic event. Use open ended questions so Mary can tell her story and describe what is troubling her.

Addressing Mary's needs to connect with family and community are very important. Suppose she asks you questions about what is going on, about what has happened, and what will be happening next. It is likely that such questions reflect concern about reaching her family, friends, or those on whom she is dependent. She may also be expressing worry about her pets, her home, and her possessions. Inquire about what things concern her about what has happened, about who might be worried about her, and about how she would like to let others know she is alright. During your discussion with Mary, it would be well to make note of her mental status and orientation, and to attend to potential risks such as suicide, substance abuse, or medication withdrawal. Mary's withdrawal and mutism are potentially serious; if you can, ask about these reactions.

Assume that we determine that Mary is exhibiting stress reactions and is easily frightened despite her somewhat apathetic demeanor. Also assume that we find that she has family with whom she is close; that she has no psychiatric history and that she does not seem to be hallucinating or delusional. Your task then becomes connecting her to the those resources that will provide shelter and help her locate her family.

It is important to pay attention to little things. For example, assume that while you are talking with Mary you notice she shivers when a draft of wind enters the shelter. Knowing that at this stage physical comfort serves as psychological comfort, you might offer Mary information on where she can find a blanket and encourage her to get one. This simple task may help Mary meet other people (e.g., she is likely have a brief interaction with the volunteer who is overseeing blanket distribution), it provides a task on which to focus, and it provides her with a sense of control in that it is her decision about whether she chooses to go get a blanket. Before you move on to the next survivor, you should offer Mary a handout that lists the resources available to her.

It is early in the postattack time frame. The support, attention, and psychological first aid you have just provided has given you as much information as you need at this time. Mary does not seem to meet criteria for a follow-up encounter, but if you continue to be concerned about her sullen and mute response to people, you may ask Mary if it would be alright if you (or someone else) check in with her in a few days to see how she is doing. When she agrees, you should take down her contact information. Because the terrorist attack occurred in a nonresidential area, she will likely be able to return to her home and family within a relatively short period of time.

Following your initial interaction with Mary, the following contacts might occur. Within the next two weeks, you or another volunteer should make a follow-up phone call to Mary, assuming that you have put her on a follow up list. She might report feeling a little "jumpy" and indicate that she has nightmares three times a week. She might report "feeling very alone." If she has not returned to work and continues to have these high stress signs, or is failing to meet her personal responsibilities, she should be offered the second stage of intervention. Given her wariness, face to face contact will be helpful to establish a relationship that might help anchor her through the difficulties that she faces. If she were able to establish a working and collaborative relationship somewhat easier, it is possible that she could be given the second stage intervention via telephone. Intervention would continue for a few sessions until she either did not endorse any of the critical questions about symptoms or agreed to enter the more extensive treatments at Stage 3. If she does not want to enter Stage 3 intervention, she should be provided with instruction about when it might be appropriate to seek additional assistance and given the contact information for available resources should she decide to seek out such services at a later date.

Vignette 2: Bill

Bill is a single, 35 year old Caucasian male 9/11 survivor of the twin towers; he has been flagged for follow-up through Stages 1 and 2 for reporting recurring intrusive thoughts and memories and hyperarousal, including an exaggerated startle response, insomnia, and hyper-vigilance. He reports having been the victim of a physical assault when he was mugged in adolescence. Bill has limited social support, has withdrawn from his normal routine and reports not wanting to leave his home. He has also reported an increase in alcohol consumption, because whiskey is the only thing that helps him "chill out a little and get a break from my mind." It is now 14 weeks after the attack, and Bill has been referred for Stage 3 treatment. He has agreed to take advantage of the opportunity for additional assistance because his sister encouraged him to do so.

During the initial counseling contact with Bill, the mental health responder commented on Bill's willingness to talk. Bill seemed responsive and asked about Stage 3 counseling. The mental health worker took time to explain what might happen in counseling, stressed the importance of finding out more about his continuing reactions, and normalized help-seeking. However, it soon became clear that Bill met the criteria for a diagnosis of PTSD.

Comment

Your task at this point is to educate Bill about the symptoms and nature of stress, and explore how he has been coping with since 9/11. This leads to a discussion about alcohol use. Bill denies drinking heavily before the terrorist events, but does acknowledge now drinking nightly "to cope." Either through a semistructured interview or through some self-report measures, you should then seek to identify several dimensions that will help you select and apply an effective treatment. You will want to assess Bill's coping style, his level of impairment, and his ability to cooperate with treatment recommendations (i.e., his level of resistance). Let's assume that Bill's premorbid history suggests that he is an externalizer who tends to avoid conflict by isolating himself, feeling victimized, and becoming resentful. He tends to act in passive-aggressive ways and occasionally has outbursts of anger.

Moreover, assume that he now meets the criteria for diagnoses of alcohol dependency and depression. You note that Bill has moderate impairment in functioning, and he has lost a job recently because of his temper. Further, your review of his history convinces you that he is mildly oppositional and resistant. Your task at this point is to present a treatment plan that will not be rejected. It should include close monitoring, because of his impairment level, and should focus on problematic symptoms associated with drinking and depression, consistent with this client's coping style. His level of resistance is quite low and he seems to gravitate to direction, so your intervention can be therapist led.

With these conclusions in mind, you initiate a program that emphasizes symptom control and skill building. After a discussion of the pros and cons of drinking, Bill might be willing to agree to reduce his alcohol consumption. This would allow you to set some mutual goals for doing so. To intensify treatment, you may encourage Bill to join Alcoholics Anonymous, and you may want to supplement your regular contact with him with telephone follow ups one or two times per week.

In the next therapy session, Bill will learn coping strategies, including relaxation training and self-monitoring. With close monitoring, this should result in a reduction of his drinking, and a resumption of some of his previous routines. His externalizing coping style will not make him a good candidate for exposure treatment, but he may benefit from participation in social groups or self-help groups.

6

Further Reading

Some Useful Websites

National Center for PTSD
   (www.ncptsd.va.gov)
   This site provides a wealth of information on stress reactions and psychological first aid,
   and it includes fact sheets that can be distributed publicly.

National Child Traumatic Stress Network
   (http://www.nctsnet.org/nccts/nav.do?pid=hom_main)
   This site provides information on children and trauma.

National Center on the Psychology of Terrorism
   (http://www.terrorismpsychology.org)
   The National Center on the Psychology of Terrorism received the American Psychological
   Association's *Award for Innovative Graduate Training Program in Clinical Psychology*.
   A visit to this site will provide links to publications and technical reports and descrip-
   tions of research activities.

Center for the Study of Traumatic Stress
   (http://www.centerforthestudyoftraumaticstress.org/home.shtml)
   Here you can find fact sheets as well as information about traumatic stress and terrorism
   preparedness.

International Society for Traumatic Stress Studies
   (www.istss.org)
   An international leader on traumatic stress, ISTSS offers a variety of information relat-
   ing to trauma.

SAMHSA's Disaster Technical Assistance Center
   (http://www.mentalhealth.samhsa.gov/dtac/default.asp)
   In addition to information on disaster mental health, this site includes links to *Mental
   Health Response for Mass Violence and Terrorism: A Field Guide*, which offers information a variety of topics, including special populations.

VA-Department of Defense Clinical Practice Guideline for Management of Traumatic Stress
   (http://www.oqp.med.va.gov/cpg/PTSD/PTSD_Base.htm)
   Offers clinical practice guidelines for traumatic stress.

Palo Alto Medical Reserve Corps (PAMRC)
   (http://www.paloaltomrc.com)
   Offers information about the Palo Alto Medical Reserve Corps; an organization that
   provides education and training for mental health practitioners, first responders and the
   general public.

Books and Articles

Castonguay, L. G., & Beutler, L. E. (Eds.) (2006). *Principles of treatment change that work*. New York: Oxford University Press.
This volume describes and discusses available research-based principles that guide treatment of anxiety disorders, depression, and chemical abuse.

Follette, V. F., & Ruzek, J. I. (2006). *Cognitive-behavioral therapies for trauma* (2nd ed.). New York: Guilford Press.
This volume provides a comprehensive review of current cognitive-behavioral interventions for acute stress problems, posttraumatic stress disorder, and other trauma-related problems (e.g., substance abuse).

Litz, B. T., Gray, M. J., Bryant, R., & Adler, A. B. (2002). Early intervention for trauma: Current status and future directions. *Clinical Psychology: Science and Practice, 9,* 112–134.
This paper offers the reader a comprehensive and thorough review of early intervention.

Litz, B. T. (2004). *Early intervention for trauma and traumatic loss*. New York: Guilford Press.
The book provides a succinct overview of current thinking related to early intervention.

McNally, R., Bryant, R. A., & Ehlers, A. (2003). Does early psychological intervention promote recovery from posttraumatic stress? *Psychological Science in the Public Interest, 4,* 45–79.
This article provides a scholarly review of the evidence related to the impact of early intervention.

National Child Traumatic Stress Network and National Center for PTSD (2005). *Psychological first aid: Field operations guide*. Available online at http://www.ncptsd.va.gov/pfa/PFA.html.

National Institute of Mental Health (2002). *Mental health and mass violence: Evidenced-based early psychological intervention for victims/survivors of mass violence. A workshop to reach consensus on best practices*. NIM Publication No. 02-5138. Washington, DC: U.S. Government Printing Office. Available online at http://www.nimh.nih.gov/publicat/massviolence.pdf)
This guide outlines a best practices model for interventions for those surviving mass violence and provides information on screening tools as well as a range of other applicable and important topics.

Norris, F. H., Friedman, M. J., Watson, P. J., Byrne, C. M., Diaz, E., & Kaniasty, K. (2002). 60,000 disaster victims speak: Part I. An empirical review of the empirical literature, 1981–2001. *Psychiatry, 65,* 207–239.
This article provides a systematic review of research on disaster survivors.

Norris, F. H., Hamblen, J. L., Watson, P. J., Ruzek, J. I., Gibson, L. E., Price, J. L. et al. (2006). Toward understanding and creating systems of postdisaster care: Findings and recommendations from a case study of New York's response to the World Trade Center disaster. In E. C. Ritchie, P. J. Watson, & M. J. Friedman (Eds.), *Mental health intervention following disasters or mass violence* (pp. 343–364). New York: Guilford Press.
Based on systematic interviews with a great number of agencies and individuals providing care to World Trade Center attack survivors, this paper summarizes lessons learned that can inform planning for future incidents.

Ruzek, J. I. (2006). Bringing cognitive-behavioral psychology to bear on early intervention with trauma survivors: Accident, assault, war, disaster, mass violence, and terrorism. In V. F. Follette & J. I. Ruzek (Eds.), *Cognitive-behavioral therapies for trauma* (2nd ed.). New York: Guilford Press.
This article explores the implications of cognitive-behavioral psychology for the design of early interventions for trauma survivors.

Young, B. H., Ruzek, J. I., Wong, M., Salzer, B., & Naturale, A. (2006). Disaster mental health training: Guidelines, considerations, and recommendations. In E. C. Ritchie, P. J. Watson, & M. J. Friedman (Eds.), *Mental health intervention following disasters and mass violence* (pp. 54–79). New York: Guilford.
This article gives a comprehensive look at the issues related to training mental health responders. PFA manual.

7

References

American Psychiatric Association, & American Psychiatric Association. Task Force on DSM-IV. (2000). *Diagnostic and statistical manual of mental disorders : DSM-IV-TR* (4th ed.). Washington, DC: American Psychiatric Association.

Andrews, B., Brewin, C. R., Rose, S., & Kirk, M. (2000) Predicting PTSD symptoms in victims of violent crime: The role of shame, anger, and childhood abuse. *Journal of Abnormal Psychology, 109,* 69–73.

Benight, C. C., & Bandura, A. (2004). Social cognitive theory of posttraumatic recovery: the role of perceived self-efficacy. Behaviour *Research and Therapy, 42,* 1129–1148.

Beutler, L. E., Clarkin, J. F., & Bongar, B. (2000). *Guidelines for the systematic treatment of the depressed patient.* New York: Oxford University Press.

Beutler, L. E., Consoli, A. J., & Lane, G. (2005). Systematic treatment selection and pre-scriptive psychotherapy. In J. Norcross, & M. J. Goldfried, (Eds), *Handbook of psychotherapy integration* (2nd ed.) (pp. 121–143). New York: Basic Books, Inc.

Beutler, L. E., & Groth-Marnat, G. (Eds)(2003). *Integrative assessment of adult personality* (2nd ed.). New York: Guilford Press.

Beutler, L. E., & Harwood, T. M. (2000). *Prescriptive psychotherapy.* New York: Guilford Press.

Beutler, L. E., Moleiro, C., Malik, M., Harwood, T.M., Romanelli, R., Gallagher-Thompson, D., & Thompson, L. (2003). A comparison of the Dodo, EST, and ATI indicators among comorbid stimulant dependent, depressed patients. *Clinical Psychology & Psychotherapy, 10,* 69–85.

Beutler, L. E., Reyes, G., Franco, Z., & Housley, J. (in press). The need for proficient mental health professionals. In L. Brown, B. Bongar, L. Pratchett, L. E. Beutler, P. Zimbardo, & J. Breckenridge (Eds), *The psychology of terrorism.* New York: Oxford University Press.

Bisson, J. I., Shepherd, J. P., Joy, D., Probert, R., & Newcombe, R. G. (2004). Early cognitive-behavioural therapy for posttraumatic stress symptoms after physical injury: Randomised controlled trial. *British Journal of Psychiatry, 184,* 63–69.

Brewin, C. R., Andrews, B, Rose, S., & Kirk, M. (1999). Acute stress disorder and post-traumatic stress disorder in victims of violent crime. *American Journal of Psychiatry, 156,* 360–366.

Brewin, C. R., Andrews, B., & Valentine, J. D. (2000). Meta-analysis of risk factors for posttraumatic stress disorder in trauma-exposed adults. *Journal of Consulting and Clinical Psychology, 68*(5), 748–766.

Bryant, R. A., A. G. Harvey, Dang, S. T., Sackville, T., & Basten, C. (1998). Treatment of acute stress disorder: A comparison of cognitive behavioral therapy and supportive counseling. *Journal of Consulting and Clinical Psychology, 66*(5), 862–866.

Bryant, R. A., Sackville, T., Dang, S. T., Moulds, M., & Guthrie, R. (1999). Treating acute stress disorder: An evaluation of cognitive behavior therapy and supportive counseling techniques. *American Journal of Psychiatry, 156*(11), 1780–1786.

Bryant, R. A., Harvey, A. G., Guthrie, R. M., & Moulds, M. L. (2000). A prospective study of psychophysiological arousal, acute stress disorder and posttraumatic stress disorder. *Journal of Abnormal Psychology, 109*(2), 341–344.

Bryant, R. A. (2003). Early predictors of posttraumatic stress disorder. *Biological Psychiatry, 53*(9), 789–795.

Brewin, C. R., Andrews, B., & Valentine, J. D. (2000). Meta-analysis of risk factors for posttraumatic stress disorder in trauma-exposed adults. *Journal of Consulting and Clinical Psychology, 68*(5), 748–766.

Brewin, C.R., Rose, S., Andrews, B., Green, J., Tata, P., McEvedy, C. et al. (2002). Brief screening instrument for post-traumatic stress disorder. *British Journal of Psychiatry, 181*(2), 158–162.

Bryant, R. A. (2003). Early predictors of posttraumatic stress disorder. *Biological Psychiatry 53*(9), 789–795.

Bryant, R. A., Harvey, A. G., Guthrie, R. M., & Moulds, M. L. (2003). Acute psychological arousal and posttraumatic stress disorder A two-year prospective study. *Journal of Traumatic Stress, 16*(5), 439–443.

Bryant, R. A., Moulds, M. L., Guthrie, R. M, Dang, S. T, & Nixon, R. D. V. (2003). Imaginal exposure alone and imaginal exposure with cognitive restructuring in treatment of posttraumatic stress disorder. *Journal of Consulting and Clinical Psychology, 71*(4), 706–712.

Castonguay, L. G., & Beutler, L. E. (Eds.) (2006a). *Principles of therapeutic change that work: Integrating relationship, treatment, client, and therapist factors.* New York: Oxford University Press.

Castonguay, L. G., & Beutler, L. E. (2006b). Common and unique principles of therapeutic change: What do we know and what do we need to know? In L. G., Castonguay & L. E. Beutler (Eds). *Principles of therapeutic change that work* (pp. 353–369). New York: Oxford University Press.

Chambless, D. L., & Ollendick, T. H. (2001). Empirically supported psychological interventions: Controversies and evidence. *Annual Review of Psychology, 52,* 685–716.

Dunmore, E.C., David, M., & Ehlers, A. (2001). A prospective investigation of the role of cognitive factors in persistent posttraumatic stress disorder (PTSD) after physical or sexual assault. *Behaviour Research and Therapy, 39*(9), 1063–1084.

Ehlers, A., & Clark, D. M. (2000). A cognitive model of posttraumatic stress disorder. *Behaviour Research and Therapy, 38,* 319–345.

Ehlers, A., & Steil, R. (1995, July). An experimental study of intrusive memories. Paper presented at the World Congress of Behavioural and Cognitive Therapies, Copenhagen, Denmark.

Ehlers, A., & Clark, D. M. (2003). Early psychological interventions for adult survivors of trauma: A review. *Society of Biological Psychiatry, 53,* 817–826.

Ehlers, A., Clark, D. M., Hackman, A., McManus, F., Fennell, M., Herbert, C, & Mayou, R. (2003). A randomized controlled trial of cognitive therapy, a self-help booklet, and repeated assessments as early interventions for posttraumatic stress disorder. *Archives of General Psychiatry, 60*(10), 1024–1032.

Fairbrother, G., Stuber, J., Galea, S., Fleishman, A. R., & Pfefferbaum, B. (2003). Posttraumatic stress reactions in New York City children after the September 11, 2001, terrorist attacks. *Ambulatory Pediatrics, 3*(6), 304–311.

Foa, E. B. (1997). Psychological processes related to recovery from a trauma and an effective treatment for PTSD. In R. Yehuda & A. C. McFarlane (Eds.), *Psychobiology of posttraumatic stress disorder* (pp. 410–424). New York: New York Academy of Scientists.

Foa, E. B., & Cahill, S. P. (2001). Psychological therapies: Emotional processing. In N. J. Smelser & P. B. Bates (Eds.). International Encyclopedia of the Social and Behavioral Science (pp. 12363–12369) Oxford: Elsvier.

Foa, E. B., Ehlers, A., Clark, D. M., Tollin, D. F., & Orsillo, S. M. (1999). The posttraumatic cognitions inventory (PCTI): Development and validation. *Psychological Assessment, 11*(3), 303–314.

Foa, E. B., Hearst-Ikeda, D., & Perry, K. J. (1995). Evaluation of a brief cognitive-behavioral program for the prevention of chronic PTSD in recent assault victims. *Journal of Consulting and Clinical Psychology, 63,* 948–955.

Foa, E. B., Keane, T. M., & Friedman, M. J. (2000), *Effective treatments for PTSD: Practice guidelines from the International Society for Traumatic Stress Studies.* New York: Guilford Press.

Foa, E. B., & Rothbaum, B. O. (1998). *Treating the trauma of rape: Cognitive-behavioral therapy for PTSD*. New York: Guilford Press.

Foa, E. B., Steketee, G., & Rothbaum, B. O. (1989). Behavioral/cognitive conceptualizations of post-traumatic stress disorder. *Behavior Therapy, 20*, 155–176.

Folstein, M. F., Folstein, S. E., & McHugh, P. R. (1975). "Mini-Mental State:" A practical method for grading the cognitive state of patients for the clinician. *Journal of Psychiatric Research, 12*, 189–198.

Friedman, M. J., Hamblen, J. L., Foa, E. B., & Charney, D. S. (2004). Commentary on a national longitudinal study of the psychological consequences of the September 11, 2001 terrorist attacks: Reactions, impairment, and help-seeking: fighting the psychological war on terrorism. *Psychiatry, 67*(2), 123–136.

Galea, S., Ahern, J., Resnick, H., Kilpatrick, D., Bucuvalas, M., Gold, J., & Vlahov, D. (2002). Psychological sequelae of the September 11 terrorist attacks in New York City. *New England Journal of Medicine, 346*, 982–987.

Galea, S., Resnick, H., Ahern, J., Gold, J., Bucuvalas, M., Kilpatrick, D., Stuber, J., & Vlahov, D. (2002). Posttraumatic stress disorder in Manhattan, New York City, after September 11th terrorist attacks. *Journal of Urban Health: Bulletin of the New York Academy of Medicine, 79*, 340–353.

Galea, S., Vlahov, D. Resnick, H., Ahern, J., Susser, E., Gold, J., Bucuvalas, M., & Kilpatrick, D. (2003). Trends of probable post-traumatic stress disorder in New York City after the September 11 terrorist attacks. *American Journal of Epidemiology, 158*, 514–524.

Gillespie, K., Duffy, M., Hackmann, A., & Clark, D. M. (2002). Community based cognitive therapy in the treatment of post-traumatic stress disorder following the Omagh bomb. *Behaviour Research and Therapy, 40*, 345–357.

Gist, R., & Lubin, B. (Eds.). (1999). *Response to disaster: Psychosocial, community, and ecological approaches*. Philadelphia, PA: Taylor & Francis.

Hamblen, J., Gibson, L. E., Mueser, K., Rosenberg, S., Jankowski, K., Watson, P., & Friedman, M. (2003). *The National Center for PTSD's Brief Intervention for Continuing Postdisaster Distress*. White River Junction, Vermont: National Center for PTSD.

Harvey, A. G., & Bryant, R. A. (1998). The relationship between acute stress disorder and posttraumatic stress disorder: A prospective evaluation of motor vehicle accident survivors. *Journal of Consulting and Clinical Psychology, 66*(3), 507–512.

Harwood, T. M. & Williams, O. B. (2003). Identifying treatment-relevant assessment: Systematic treatment selection. In L. E. Beutler & G. Groth-Marnat (Eds), *Integrative assessment of adult personality* (2nd ed.) (pp. 65–81). New York: Guilford Press.

Karno, M., Beutler, L. E., & Harwood, T. M. (2002). Interactions between psychotherapy process and patient attributes that predict alcohol treatment effectiveness: A preliminary report. *Addictive Behaviors, 27*, 779–797.

Karno, M. P., & Longabaugh, R. (2005). Less directiveness by therapists improves drinking outcomes of reactant clients in alcoholism treatment. *Journal of Consulting and Clinical Psychology, 73*, 262–267.

Karno, M. P., & Longabaugh, R. (2003). Patient depressive symptoms and therapist focus on emotional material: A new look at project MATCH. *Journal of Studies in Alcohol, 64*, 607–615.

Karno, M. P., & Longabaugh, R. (2004). What do we know? Process analysis and the search for a better understanding of Project Match's anger-by-treatment matching effect. *Journal of Studies in Alcohol, 65*, 501–512.

Kaiser, C. F., Sattler, D. N., & Bellack, D. R. (1996). A conservation of resources approach to a natural disaster: Sense of coherence and psychological distress. *Journal of Social Behavior & Personality, 11*(3), 459–476.

Keane, T. M., Zimering, R. T., & Caddell, J. M. (1985). A behavioral formulation of post-traumatic stress disorder in Vietnam veterans. *The Behavior Therapist, 8*, 9–12.

Kessler, R. C., McGonagle, K. A., Zhao, S., Nelson, C. B., Hughes, M., Eshleman, S., Wittchen, H., & Kendler, K. S. (1994). Lifetime and 12-month prevalence of DSM-III-R psychiatric disorders in the US: Results from the National Comorbidity Survey. *Archives of General Psychiatry, 51*, 8–19.

Kessler, R. C., Anthony, J. C., Blazer, D. G., Bromet, E., Eaton, W. W., Kendler, K., et al. (1997). The U.S. National Comorbidity Survey: Overview and future directions. *Epidemiologia e Psichiatria Sociale, 6*(1), 4–16.

Kessler, R. C., Chiu, W. T., Demler, O., & Walters, E. E. (2005). Prevalence, severity, and comorbidity of 12-month DSM-IV disorders in the National Comorbidity Survey Replication. *Archives of General Psychiatry, 62,* 617–627.

Kessler, R. C., Demler, O., Frank, R. G., Olfson, M., Pincus, H. A., Walters, E. E., Wang, P., Wells, K. B., & Zaslavsky, A. M. (2005). Prevalence and treatment of mental disorders, 1990 to 2003. *New England Journal of Medicine, 352*(24), 2515–2523.

Kilpatrick, D. G., Veronen, L. J., Resick, P. A. (1982). Psychological sequelae to rape: Assessment and treatment strategies. In D. M. Doleys, R. L. Meredith, A. R. Ciminero (Eds.). *Behavioral medicine: Assessment and treatment strategies* (pp. 473–497). New York: Plenum.

King, D. W., King, L. A., Foy, D. W., Keane, T. M., & Fairbank, J. A. (1999). Posttraumatic stress disorder in a national sample of female and male Vietnam veterans: Risk factors, war-zone stressors, and resilience-recovery variables. *Journal of Abnormal Psychology, 108,* 164–170.

Kulka, R. A., Schlenger, W.E., Fairbank, J. A., Hough, R. L., Jordan, B. K., Marmar, C. R., et al. (1990). *Trauma and the Vietnam war generation: Report of findings from the National Vietnam Veterans Readjustment Study.* New York: Brunner/Mazel.

Litz, B., & Gray, M. (2004). Early intervention for trauma in adults. In B. Litz (Ed.), *Early intervention for trauma and traumatic loss* (pp.87–111). New York: Guilford Press.

Litz, B., Gray, M., Bryant, R., & Adler, A. (2002). Early intervention for trauma: Current status and future directions. *Clinical Psychology: Science and Practice, 9*(2), 112–134.

Marmar, C. R., Weiss, D., & Metzler, T. J. (1997). The Peritraumatic Dissociative Experiences Questionnaire, in assessing psychological trauma and PTSD. In J. P. Wilson, & T. M. Keane (Eds), *A handbook for practitioners* (pp. 412–428). New York: Guilford Press.

McNally, R. J., Bryant, R. A., & Ehlers, A. (2003). Does early psychological intervention promote recovery from posttraumatic stress? *Psychological Science in the Public Interest, 4*(2), 45–79.

Murray, J., Ehlers, A., & Mayou, R. A. (2002). Dissociation and post-traumatic stress-disorder: Two prospective studies of road traffic accident survivors. *British Journal of Psychiatry, 180,* 363–368.

Narrow, W. E., Rae, D. S., Robins, L. N., & Regier, D. A. (2002). Revised prevalence estimates of mental disorders in the United States: Using a clinical significance criterion to reconcile 2 surveys' estimates. *Archives of General Psychiatry, 59,* 115–123.

Nathan, P. E., & Gorman, J. M. (Eds.). (2002). *A guide to treatments that work* (2nd ed.). New York: Oxford University Press.

National Child Traumatic Stress Network and National Center for PTSD (2005). *Psychological first aid: Field operations guide.* Available online at http://www.ncptsd.va.gov/pfa/PFA.html

National Institute for Clinical Excellence and the National Collaborating Centre for Mental Health (2005). *Post-traumatic stress disorder (PTSDP: The management of PTSD in adults and children in primary and secondary care.* London: National Institute fort Clinical Excellence.

National Institute of Mental Health (2002). *Mental health and mass violence: Evidenced-based early psychological intervention for victims/survivors of mass violence. A workshop to reach consensus on best practices.* NIMH Publication No. 02-5138. Washington, DC: U.S. Government Printing Office. (Available online at http://www.nimh.nih.gov/publicat/massviolence.pdf)

Norcross, J.C. (Ed.) (2002). *Psychotherapy relationships that work: Therapist contributions and responsiveness to patient needs.* New York: Oxford University Press.

Norcross, J., Beutler, L. E., & Levant, R. (Eds.) (2006). *Evidence based practices in mental health: Debate and dialogue on the fundamental questions.* Washington, D.C. American Psychological Association.

Ozer, E. J., Best, S. R., Lipsey, T. L., & Weiss, D. S. (2003). Predictors of posttraumatic stress disorder and symptoms in adults: A meta-analysis. *Psychological Bulletin, 129*(1), 52–73.

Regier, D. A., Kaelber, C. T., Rae, D. S., Farmer, M. E., Knauper, B., Kessler, R. C., & Norquist, G. S. (1998). Limitations of diagnostic criteria and assessment instruments for mental disorders. *Archives of General Psychiatry, 55,* 109–115.

Robins, L. N., Locke, B. Z., & Regier, D. A. (1991). An overview of psychiatric disorders in America. In L. N. Robins & D. A. Regier (Eds.), *Psychiatric disorders in America: The Epidemiologic Catchment Area Study* (pp. 328–366). New York: Free Press.

Rose, S., Brewin, C. R., Andrews, B., & Kirk, M. (1999). A randomized controlled trial of individual psychological debriefing for victims of violent crime. *Psychological Medicine, 29,* 793–799.

Rose, S., Wessely, S., & Bisson, J. (1998). *Brief psychological interventions ("debriefing") for trauma-related symptoms and prevention of posttraumatic stress disorder* (Cochrane Review). In The Cochrane Library, 2, Oxford University Press: Update Software.

Sattler, D. N., Preston, A. J., Kaiser, C. F., Olivera, V. E., Valdez, J., & Schlueter, S. (2002). Hurricane Georges: A cross-national study examining preparedness, resource loss, and psychological distress in the U.S. Virgin Islands, Puerto Rico, Dominican Republic, and the United States. *Journal of Traumatic Stress, 15,* 339–350.

Shalev, A.Y., Peri, T., Canetti, L., & Schreiber, S. (1996). Predictors of PTSD in injured trauma survivors: A prospective study. *American Journal of Psychiatry, 153,* 219–225.

Smith, M. L., Glass, G. V., & Miller, T. I. (1980). *The benefits of psychotherapy.* Baltimore: Johns Hopkins University Press.

Somer, E., Tamir, E., Maguen, S., & Litz, B. T. (2005). Brief cognitive-behavioral phone-based intervention targeting anxiety about the threat of attack: A pilot study. *Behaviour Research and Therapy, 43(5),* 669–79.

Substance Abuse and Mental Health Services Administration. (2002). *Results from the 2001 National Household Survey on Drug Abuse: Vol. II. Technical appendices and selected data tables.* Rockville, MD: Author.

VA-DoD Clinical Practice Guideline Working Group, Veterans Health Administration, Department of Veterans Affairs and Health Affairs, Department of Defense (2003). Management of post-traumatic stress. Washington, DC: Office of Quality and Performance publication 10Q-CPG/PTSD-04.

Vasterling, J. J., Brailey, K., & Constans, J. I. (1997). Assessment of intellectual resources in Gulf War veterans: Relationship to PTSD. *Assessment, 4*(1), 51–59.

Vlahov, D., Galea, S., Resnick, H., Ahern, J., Boscarino, J. A., Bucuvalas et al. (2002). Increased use of cigarettes, alcohol, and marijuana among Manhattan residents after the September 11th terrorist attacks. *American Journal of Epidemiology, 155,* 988–996.

Wampold, B. E. (2001). *The great psychotherapy debate: Models, methods, and findings.* Hillsdale, NJ: L. Erlbaum Associates.

Zatzick, D., Roy-Byrne, P., Russo, J., Rivara, F., Droesch, R., Wagner, A. et al. (2004). A randomized effectiveness trial of stepped collaborative care for acutely injured trauma survivors. *Archives of General Psychiatry, 61,* 498–506

Appendix: Tools and Resources

Tips for Creating Handouts

Do	Don't
List key information	Overload the handouts with too much information
Make it simple and concrete	Use complex words or concepts
Illustrate how the subject is applicable to the individual	Use too many colors
Design it so that it is pleasing to the eye and not too "busy"	Use a small font size to "fit it all in"
Always include a contact for additional assistance	Make it more than one page so that it requires staples
Avoid pictures or photos of potentially disturbing scenes	Forget to be mindful of potential triggers
Provide web links and sources for additional information	Use citations that may clutter a page

From: J. Housley & L.E. Beutler: *Treating Victims of Mass Disaster and Terrorism* © 2007 Hogrefe & Huber Publishers

Coping Tools Handout (Example)

Tool	Key Points	Just for Me	
		When/where to Practice	**When to Use**
Deep breathing	Inhale deeply	In my chair or bed	Before I have to make phone calls
	Exhale slowly	Before each meal	When I get upset, like when I have to talk about the disaster
	Think "relax" as you exhale	Before I go to bed each night	When I feel my body getting tense When I can't sleep When I have trouble concentrating

From: J. Housley & L.E. Beutler: *Treating Victims of Mass Disaster and Terrorism* © 2007 Hogrefe & Huber Publishers

Helpful Information Handout (Example)

Topic	Key Points	How This Will Help Me
Positive/negative coping	Everyone copes in different ways	Positive coping that I like to do includes reading, talking to friends, journaling, and exercising
	Positive coping works well over the long-term	Negative coping I will avoid includes isolating myself and using alcohol more than usual
	Negative coping can be harmful over the long-term	If I am worried about my coping, I can get help by calling this number: <list number>.

From: J. Housley & L.E. Beutler: *Treating Victims of Mass Disaster and Terrorism* © 2007 Hogrefe & Huber Publishers

Potential Psychoeducation Topics

Topic
Relationship between thoughts, emotions, and behaviors
Thought intrusions
Emotional numbing
Avoidance
Physical arousal
Loss of interest
Eating habits
Sleep hygiene
Anger management
Positive coping
Negative coping
Depression
Anxiety and worry
Difficulty concentrating
Substance abuse prevention
Social support: Giving and receiving
Problem solving

From: J. Housley & L.E. Beutler: *Treating Victims of Mass Disaster and Terrorism* © 2007 Hogrefe & Huber Publishers

Overview of Tools Associated with Each Stage

Stage	Tool	Description
1.	Presence	Be present in a calm and respectful manner
	Answering questions and providing basic information	Provide helpful and applicable information/services
	Social support	Encourage use of social support
	Brief coping advice	Educate on positive and negative coping
	Coping skills training	Offer basic information on helpful topics
2.	Supportive and collaborative environment	Foster a supportive and collaborative environment
	Communicating basis for treatment	Discuss what the purpose of the visits are
	Psychoeducation	Provide education on helpful topics
	Identifying and assessing thoughts	Assist in identifying maladaptive thoughts and evaluating those thoughts for validity
	Cognitive restructuring	Discuss the links between thoughts, emotion and behavior and determine if examining alternative views would be helpful
	Anxiety management	Instruct and practice anxiety management
	Homework	Practice, practice, practice
3. Internalizing Victims	Supportive therapy	Foster a supportive and collaborative environment
	Training to stay in the moment	Stay with dealings and be in the moment
	Self-esteem training	Capitalize on accomplishment and achievements
	Exposure	Confronting thoughts and images that produce anxiety in order to extinguish fear and reduce the sense of danger and distress over time
3. Externalizing Victims	Rationale for treatment	Explain the rationale behind treatment
	Daily activity schedule	Use to learn the relationship between thoughts and behaviors
	Thought records	Used as tool to identify unrealistic or dysfunctional patterns of thought
	Homework	Practice, practice, practice

From: J. Housley & L.E. Beutler: *Treating Victims of Mass Disaster and Terrorism*   © 2007 Hogrefe & Huber Publishers